# OCTOBER 50 COLORING PAGES FOR OLDER KIDS RELAXATION

## SHIH CHIEN HUA

PUBLISHED BY:
SHIH CHIEN HUA
Copyright © 2018

SEABIRD SHOP >50FOR

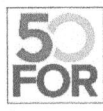

FB  FAN PAGE

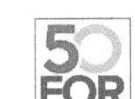

**Disclaimer**
The information contained in this book is for general information purposes only. The information is provided by the authors and while we endeavor to keep the information up to date and correct, we make no representations or warranties of any kind, express or implied, about the completeness, accuracy, reliability, suitability or availability with respect to the book or the information, products, services, or related graphics contained in the book for any purpose. Any reliance you place on such information is therefore strictly at your own risk.

# OCTOBER IST

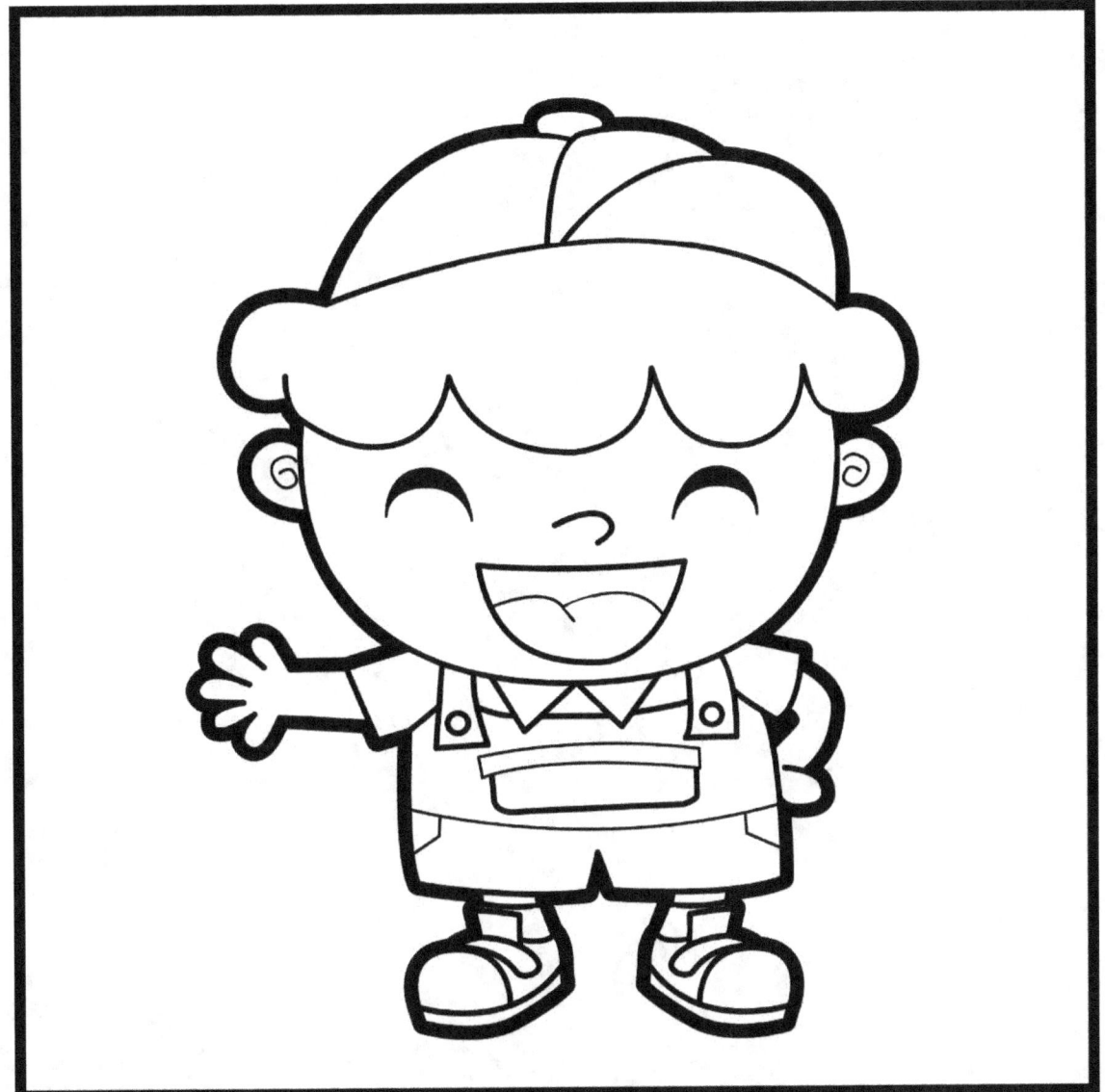

note:

_____

_____

_____

# OCTOBER 2ND

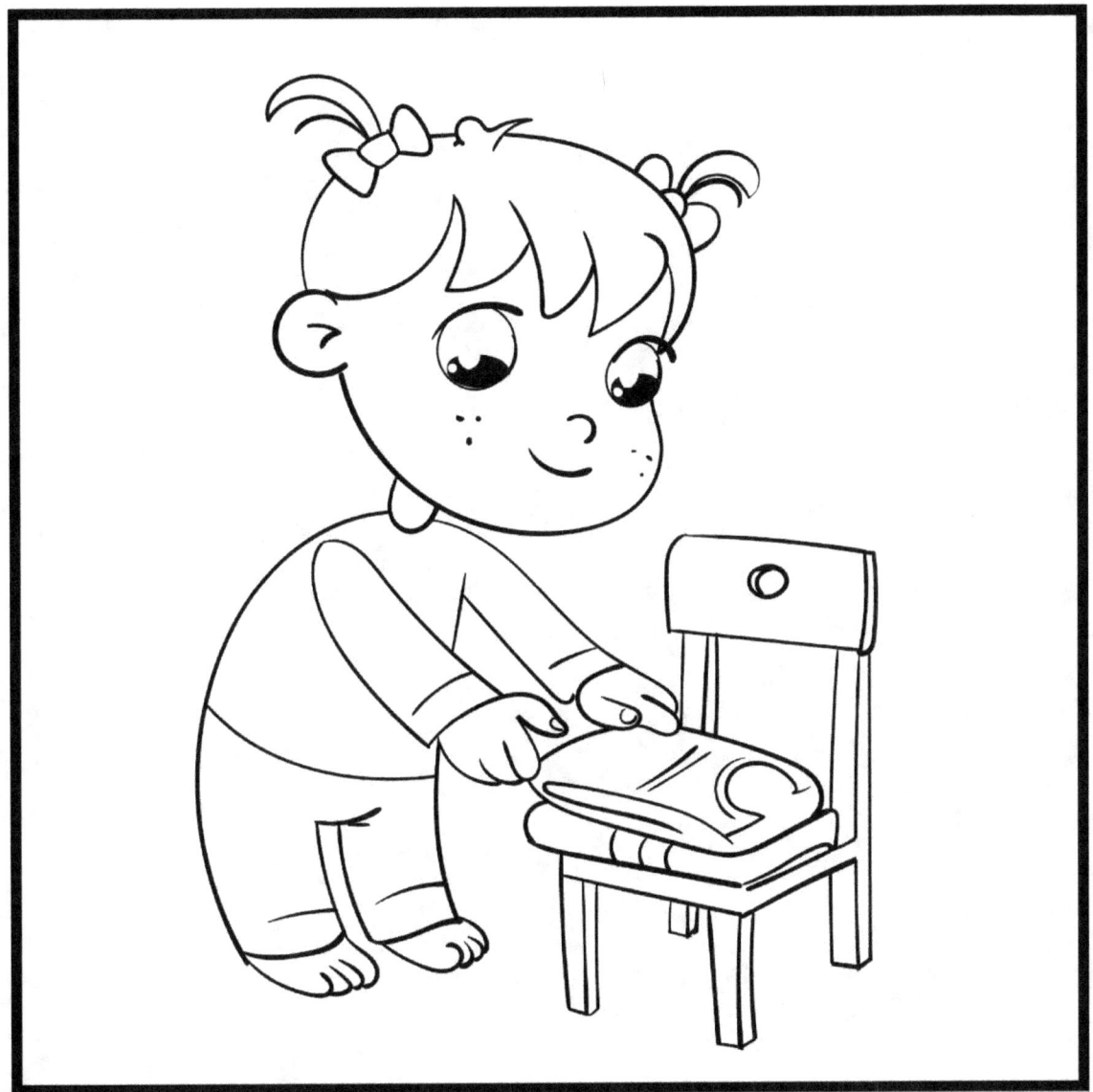

note:

_____

_____

_____

# OCTOBER 3RD

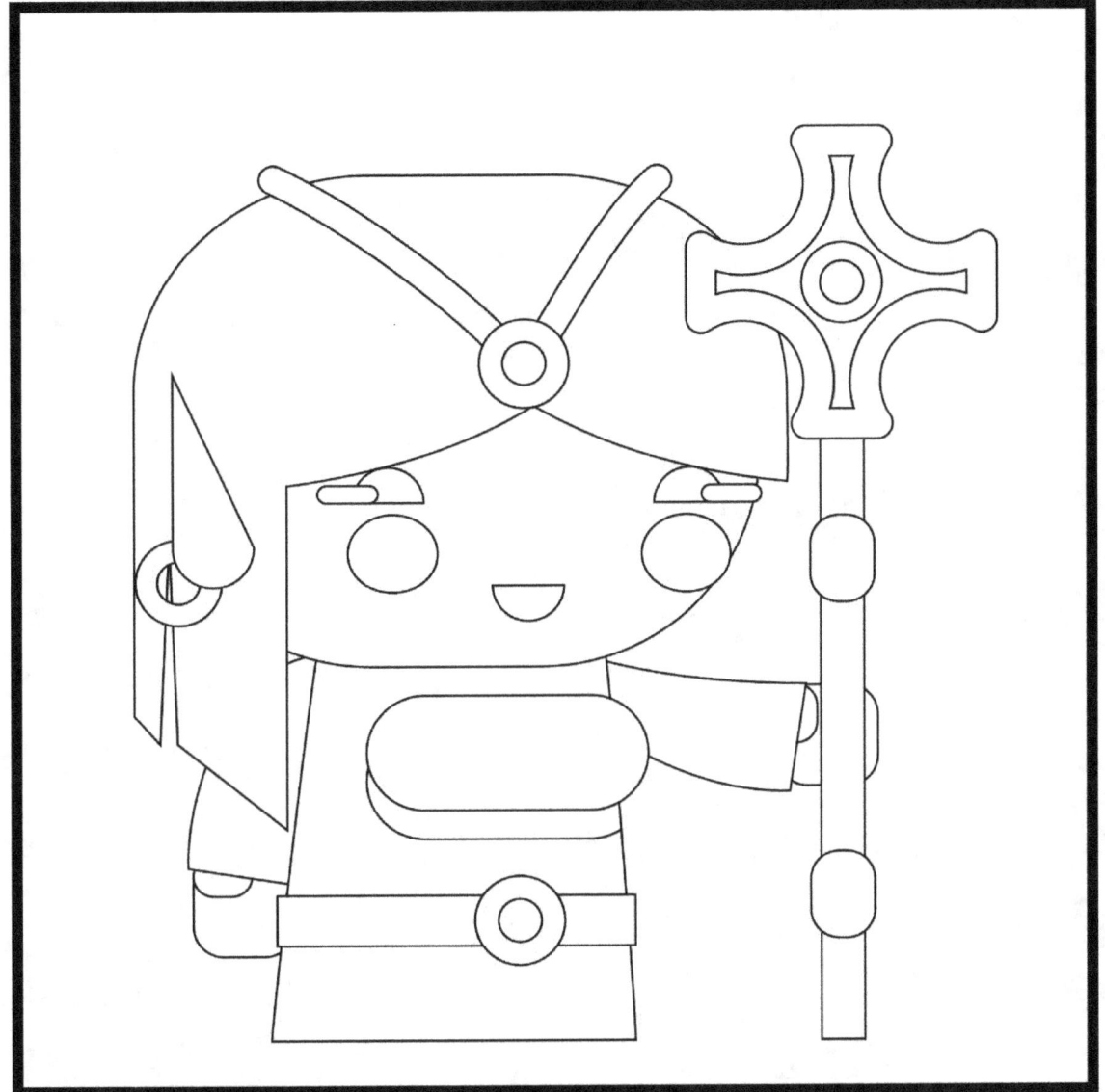

note:

_____

_____

_____

# OCTOBER 4TH

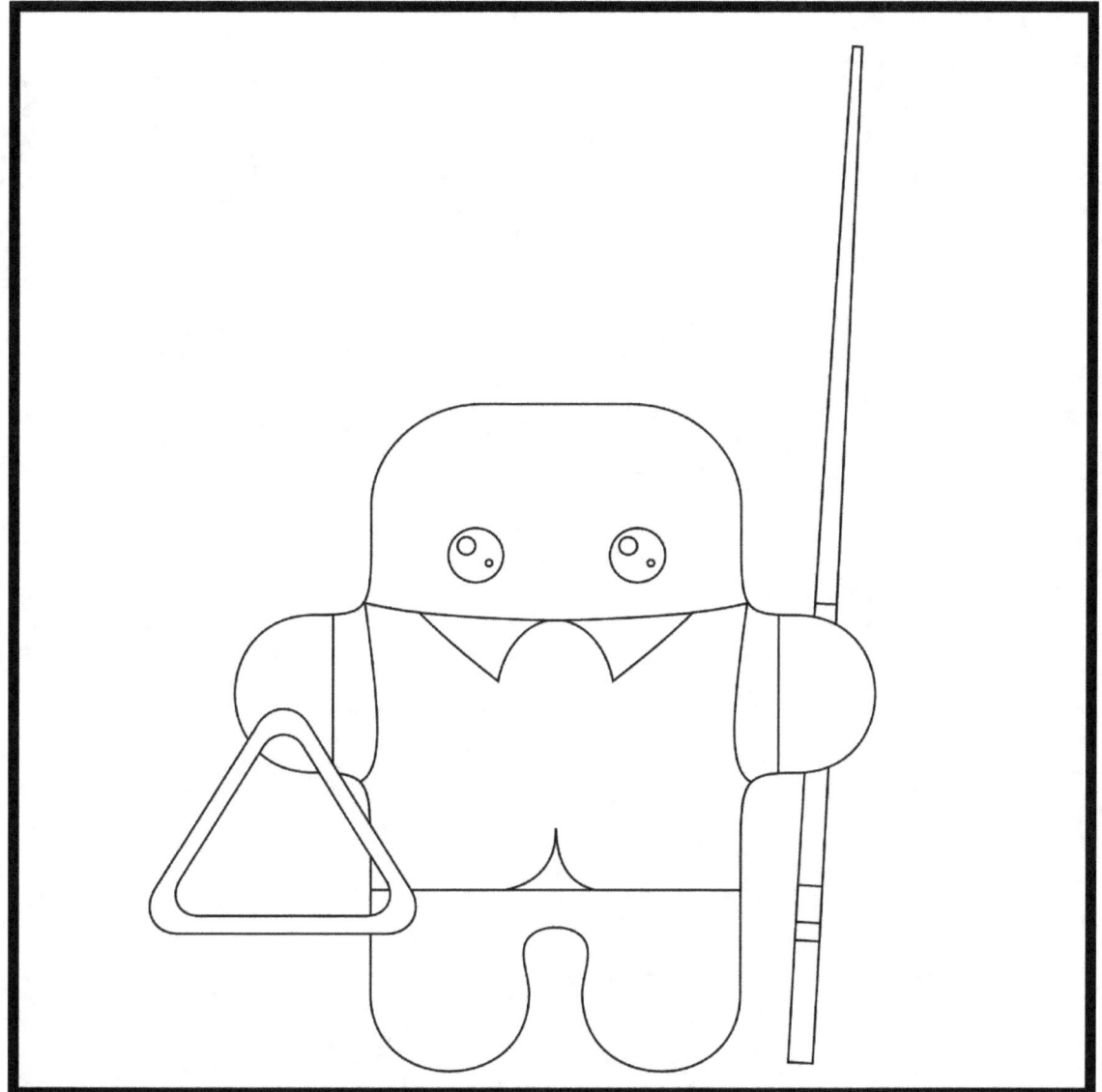

note:

_____

_____

_____

# OCTOBER 5TH

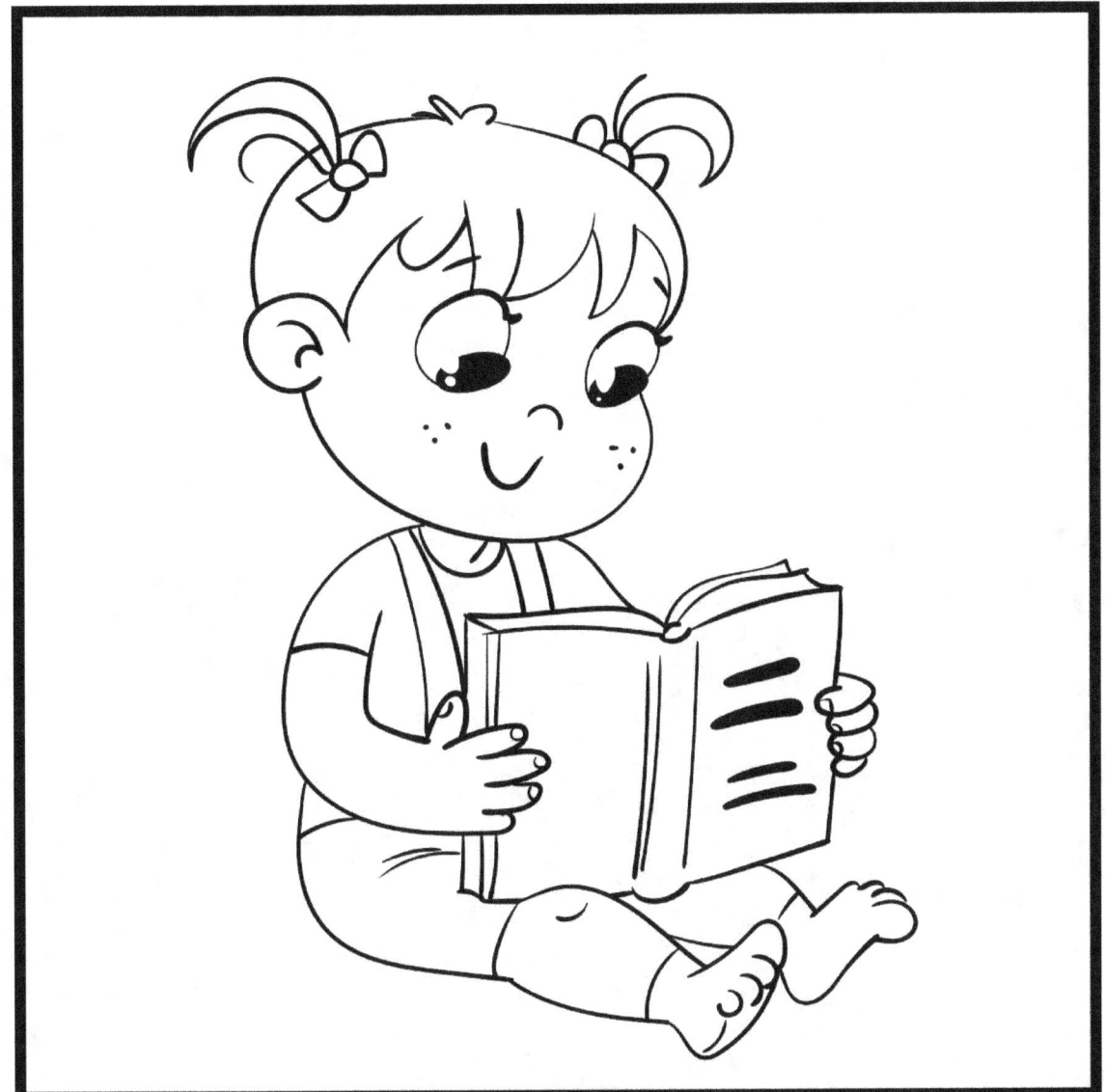

note:

_____

_____

_____

# OCTOBER 6TH

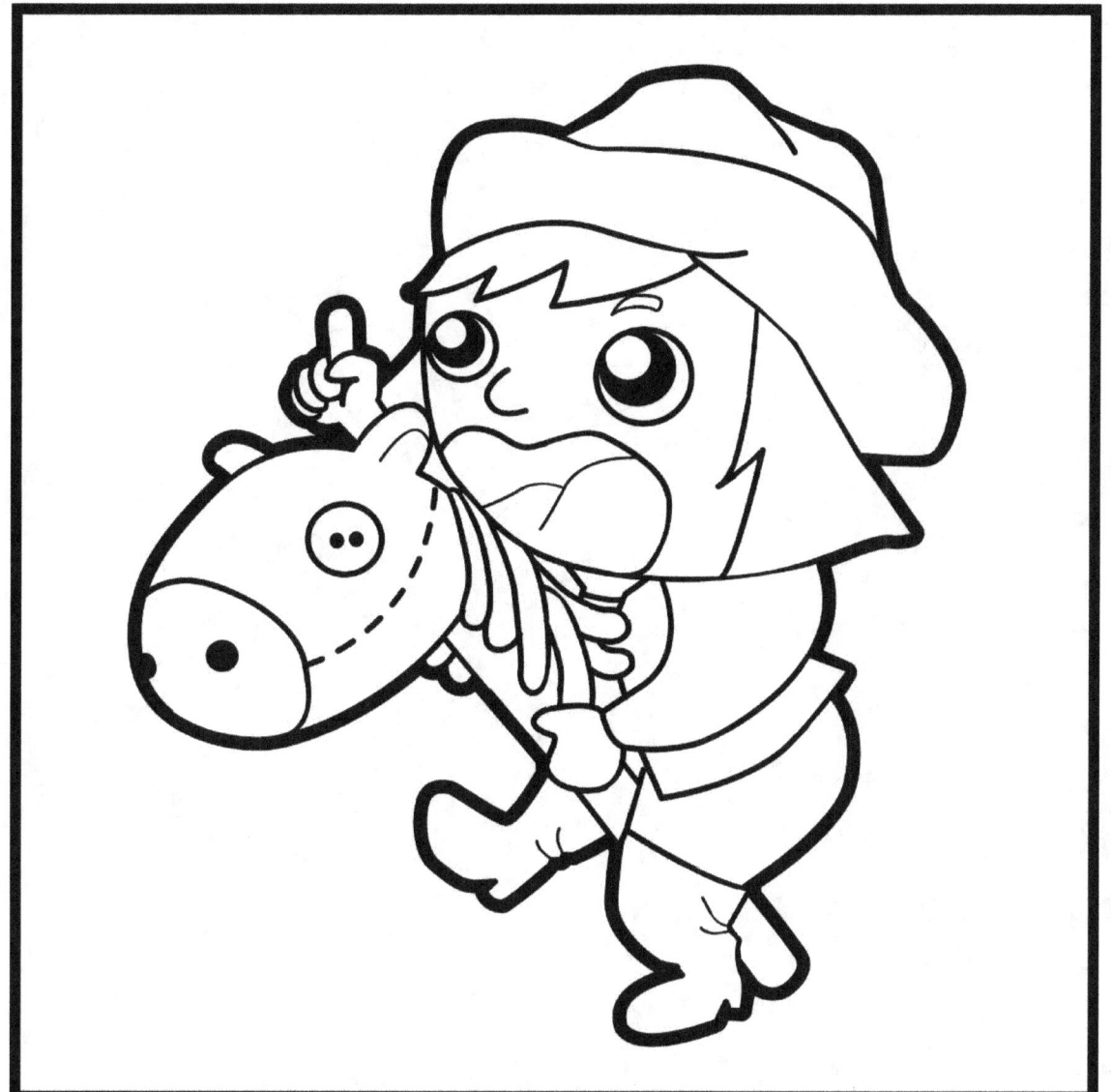

note:

_____

_____

_____

# OCTOBER 7TH

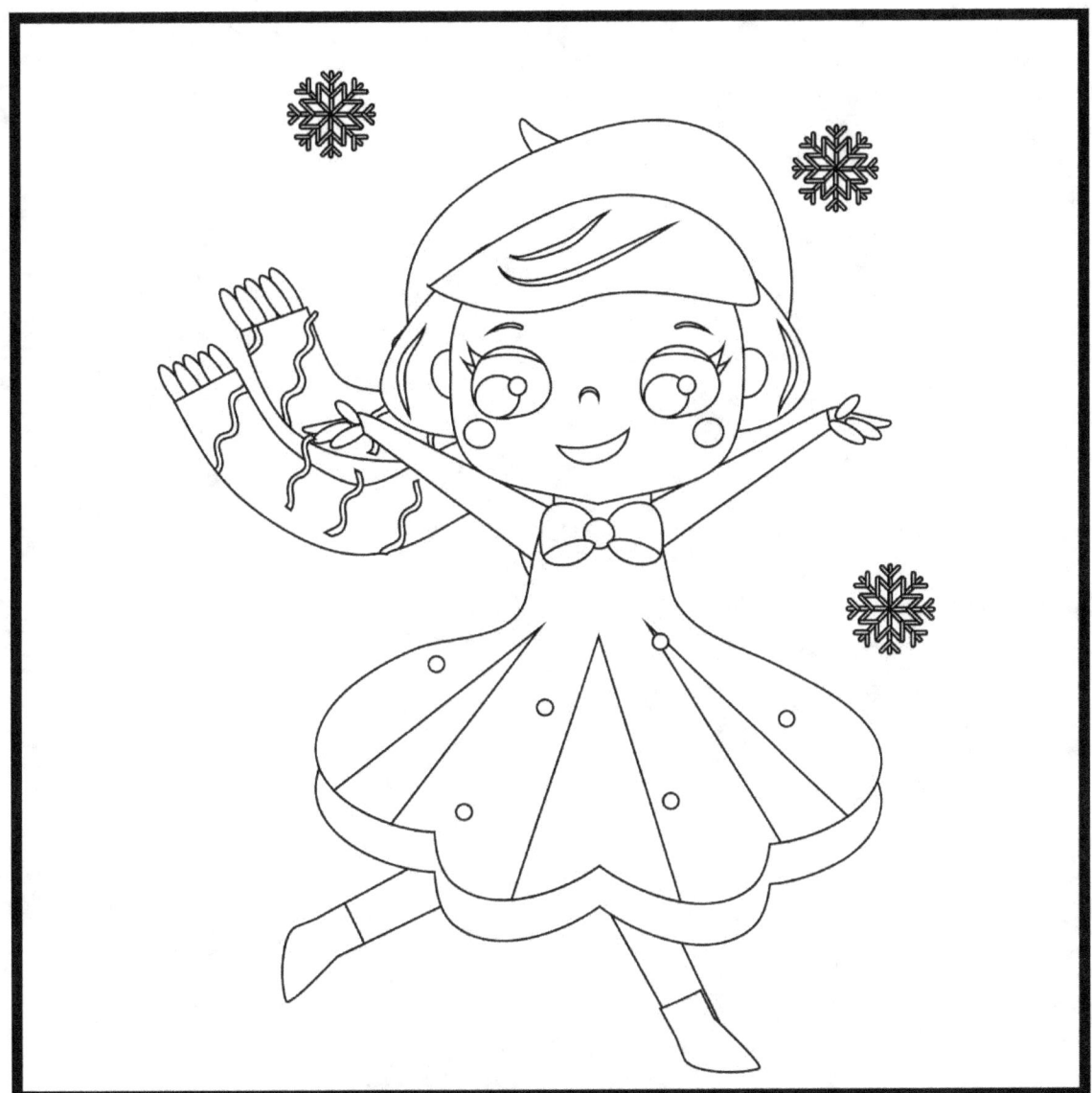

note:

_____

_____

_____

# OCTOBER 8TH

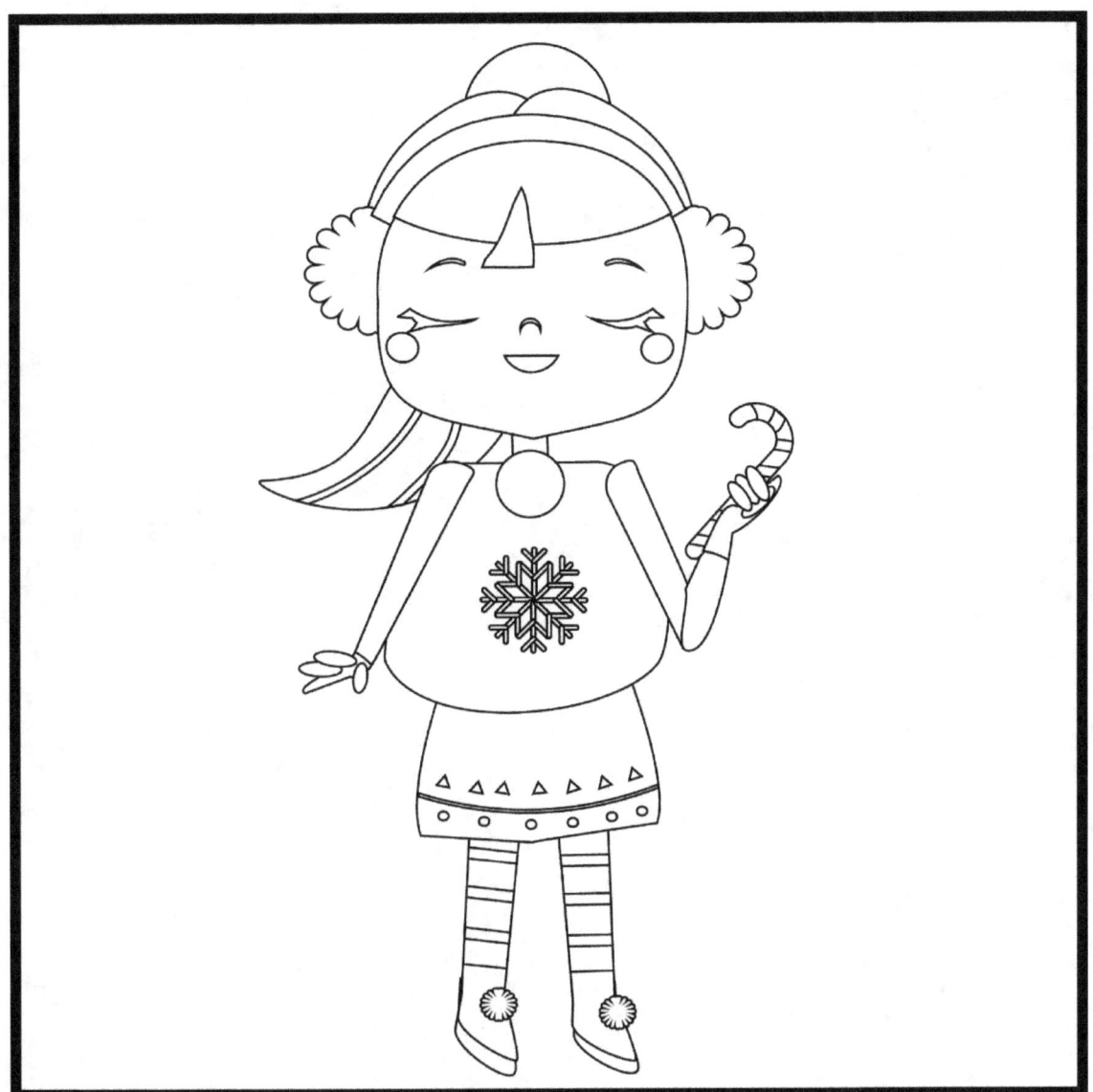

note:

_____

_____

_____

# OCTOBER 9TH

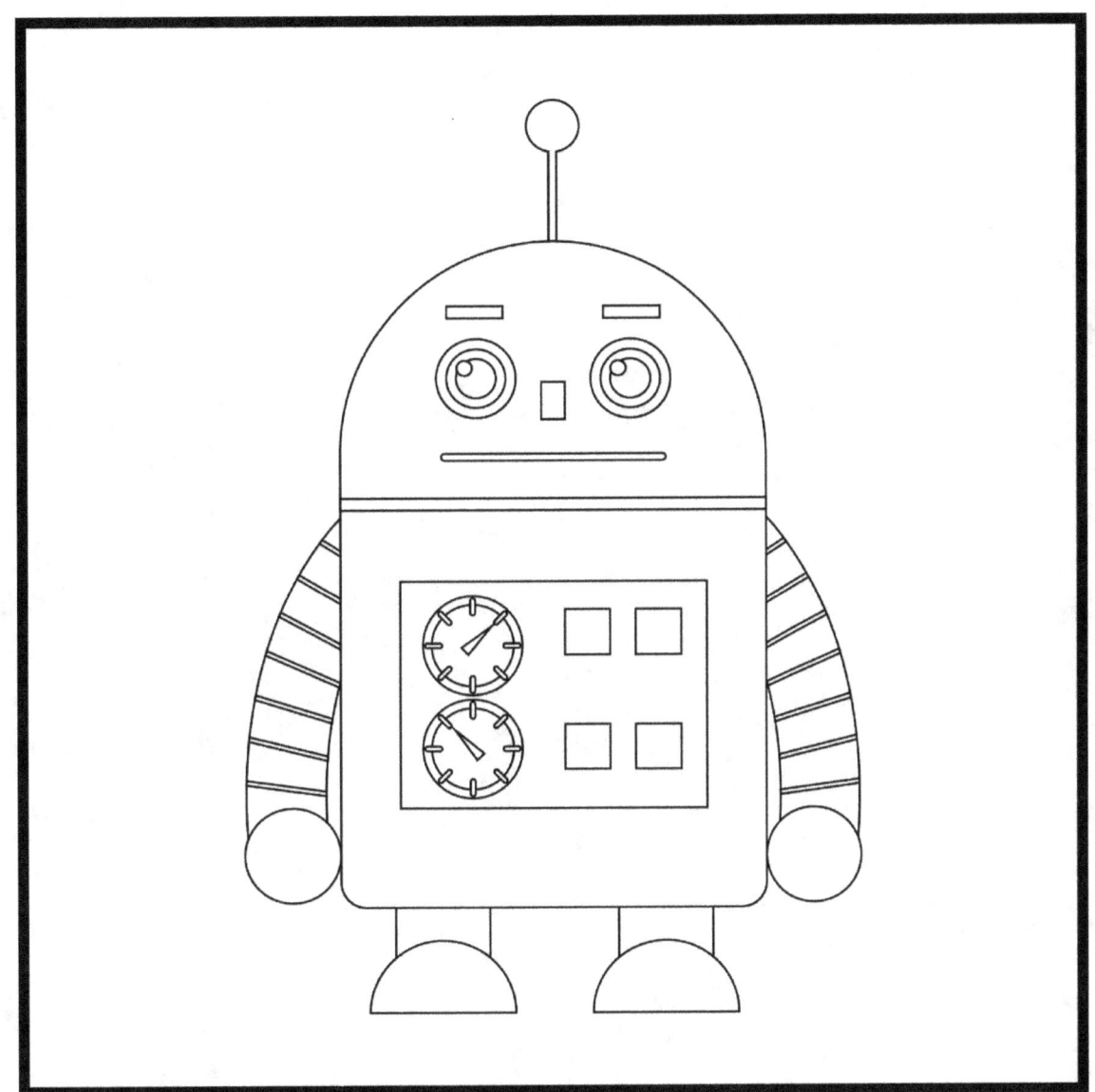

note:

_____

_____

_____

# OCTOBER 10TH

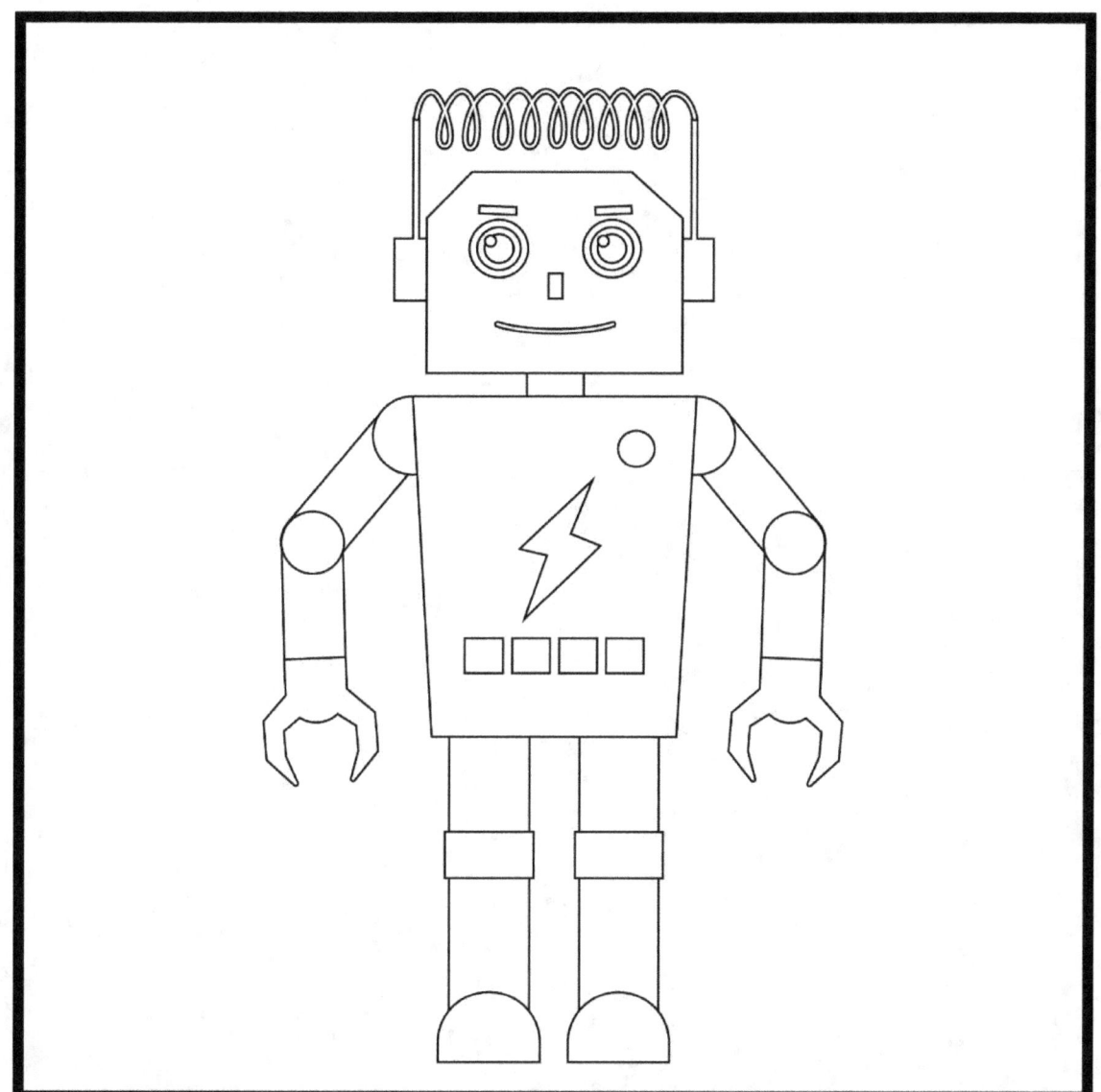

note:

_____

_____

_____

# OCTOBER 11TH

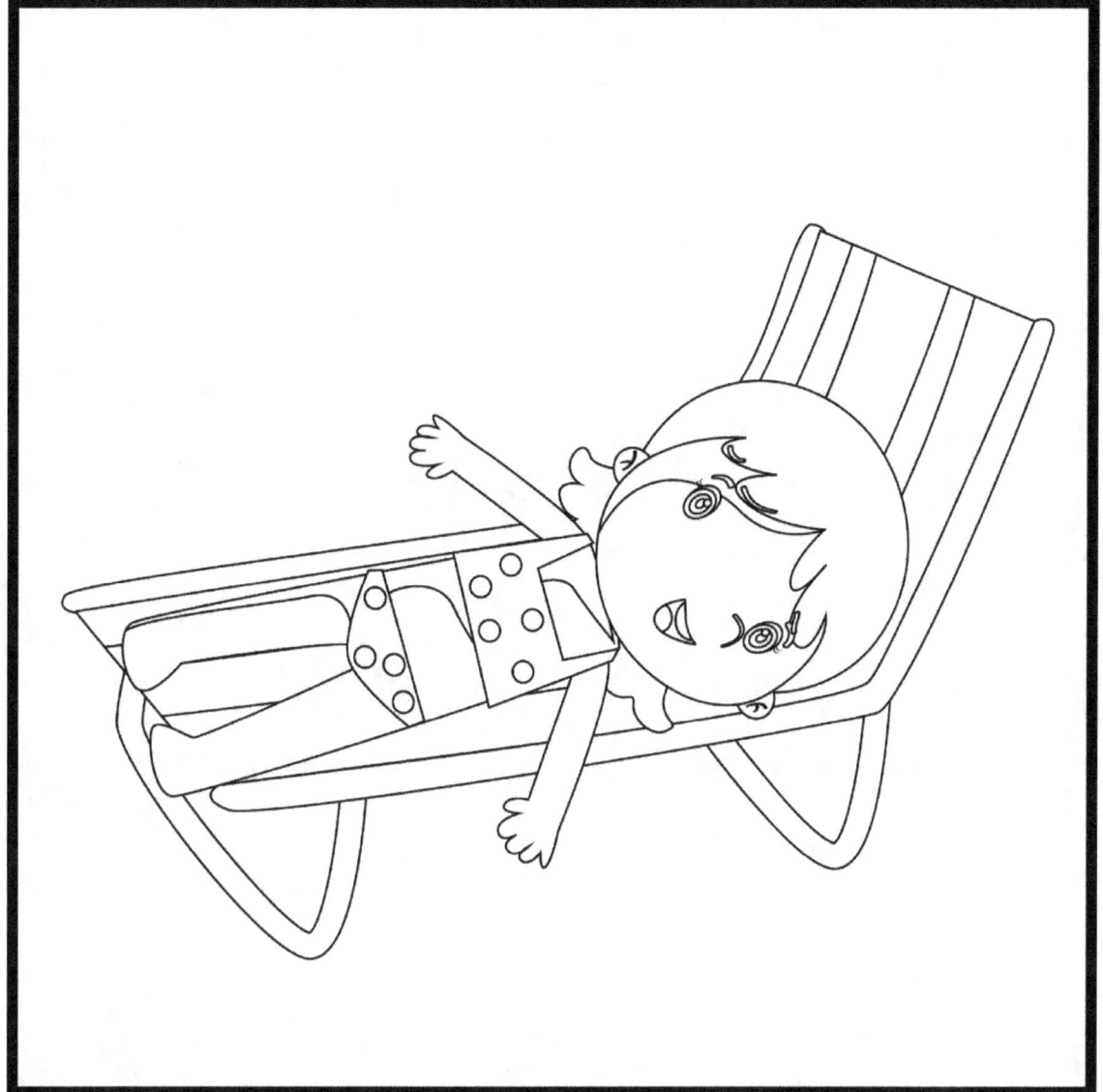

note:

_____

_____

_____

# OCTOBER 12TH

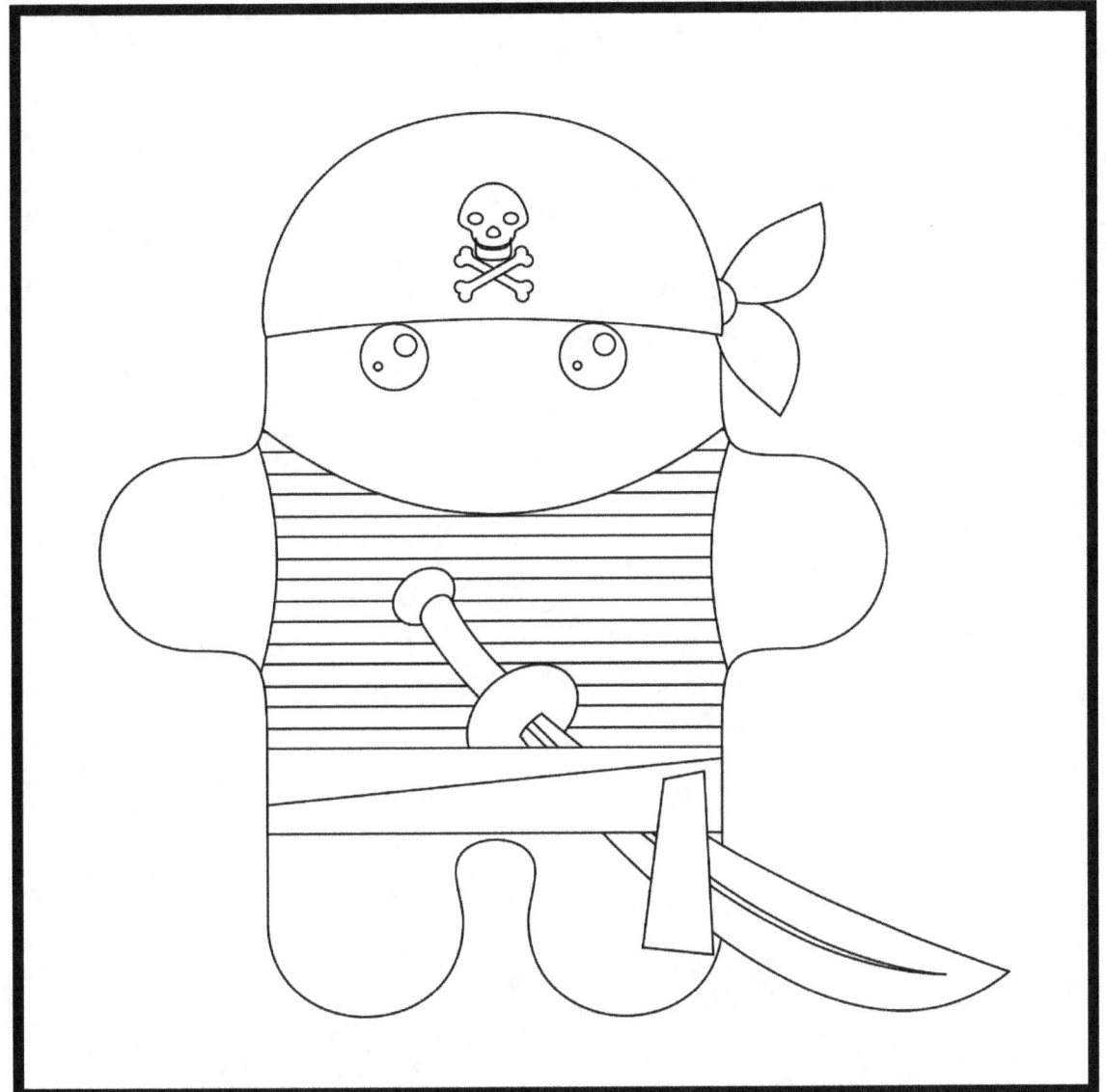

note:

_____

_____

_____

# OCTOBER 13TH

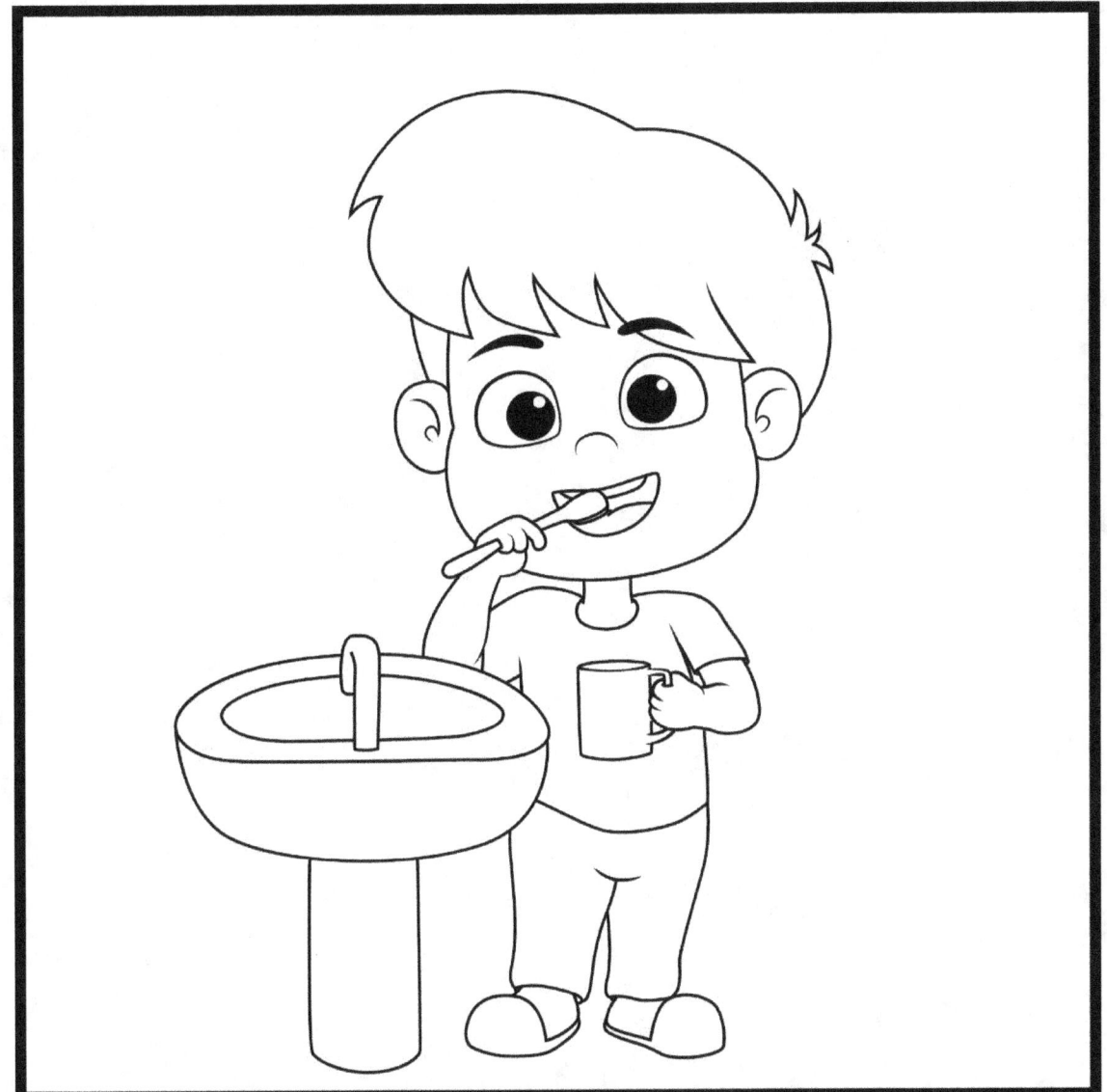

note:

_____

_____

_____

# OCTOBER 14TH

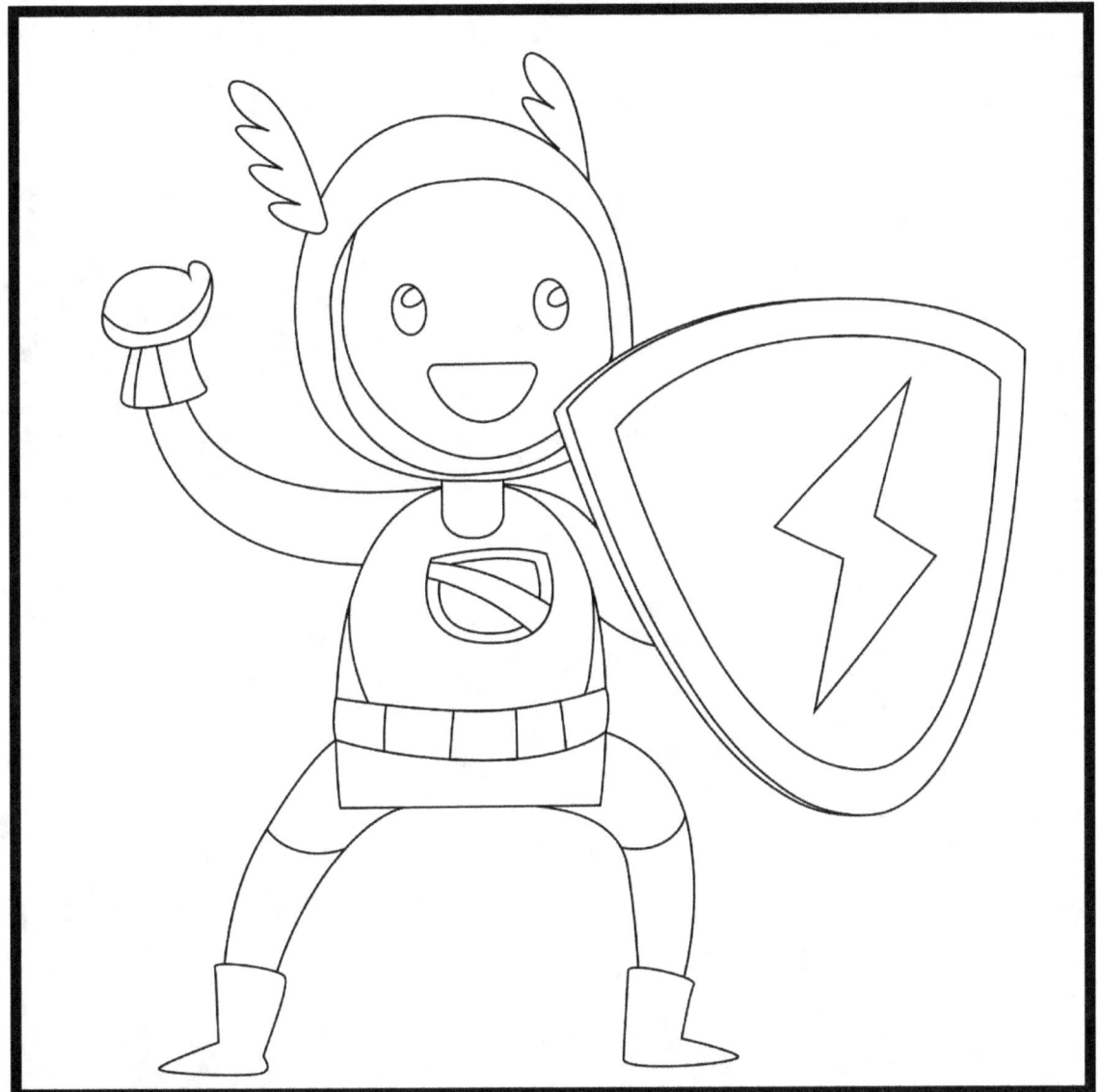

note:

_____

_____

_____

# OCTOBER 15TH

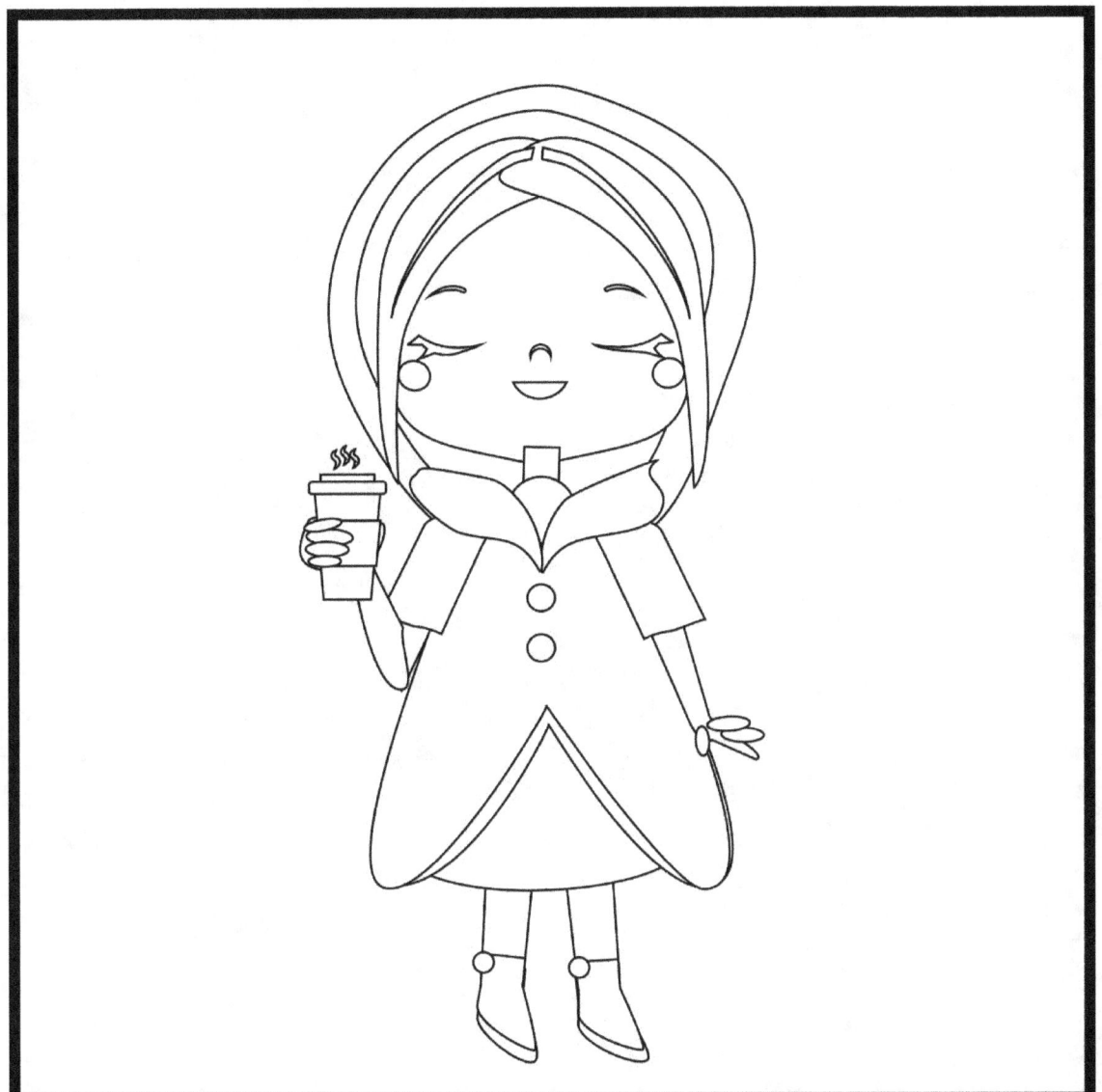

note:

_____

_____

_____

# OCTOBER 16TH

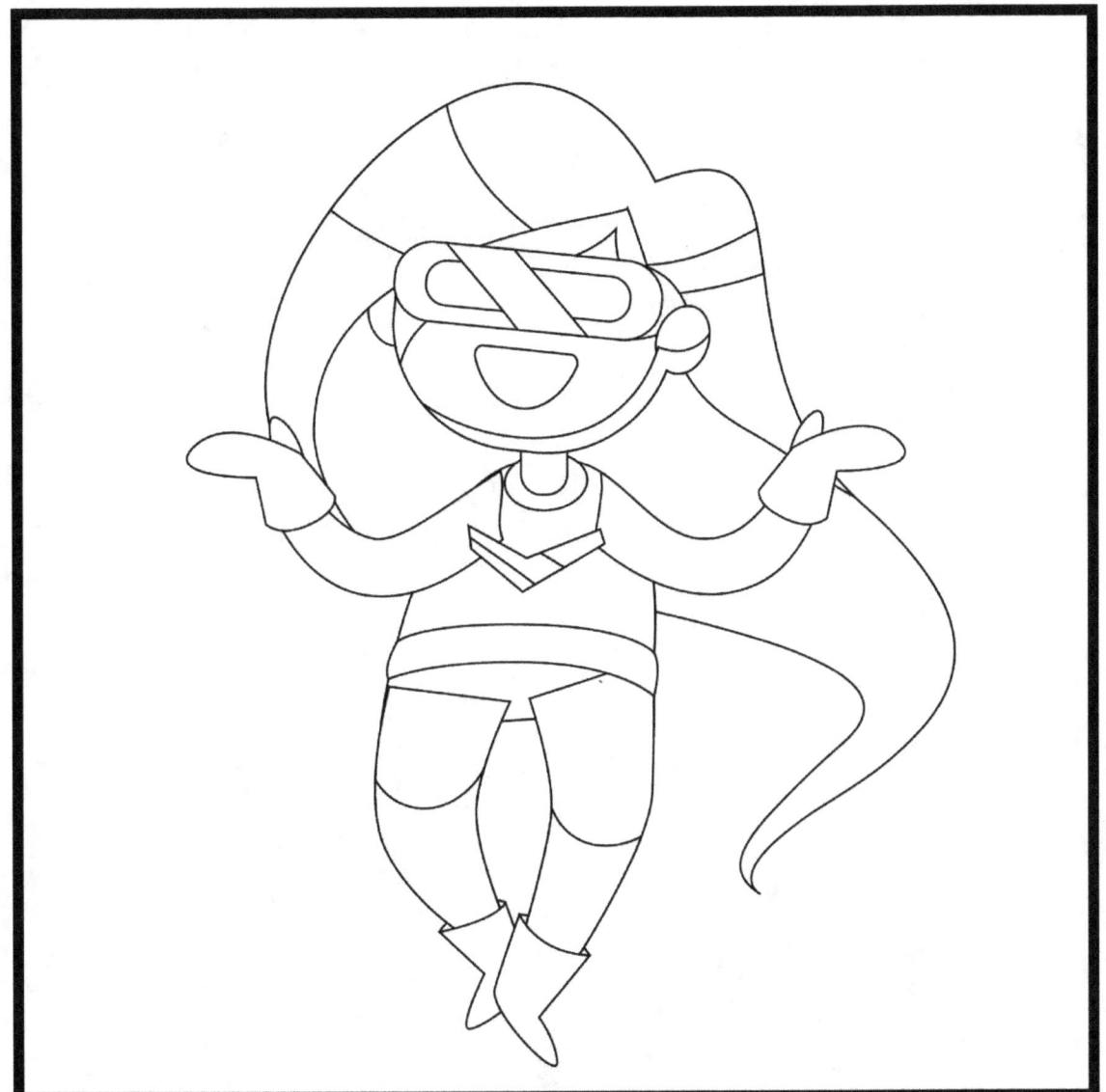

note:

_____

_____

_____

# OCTOBER 17TH

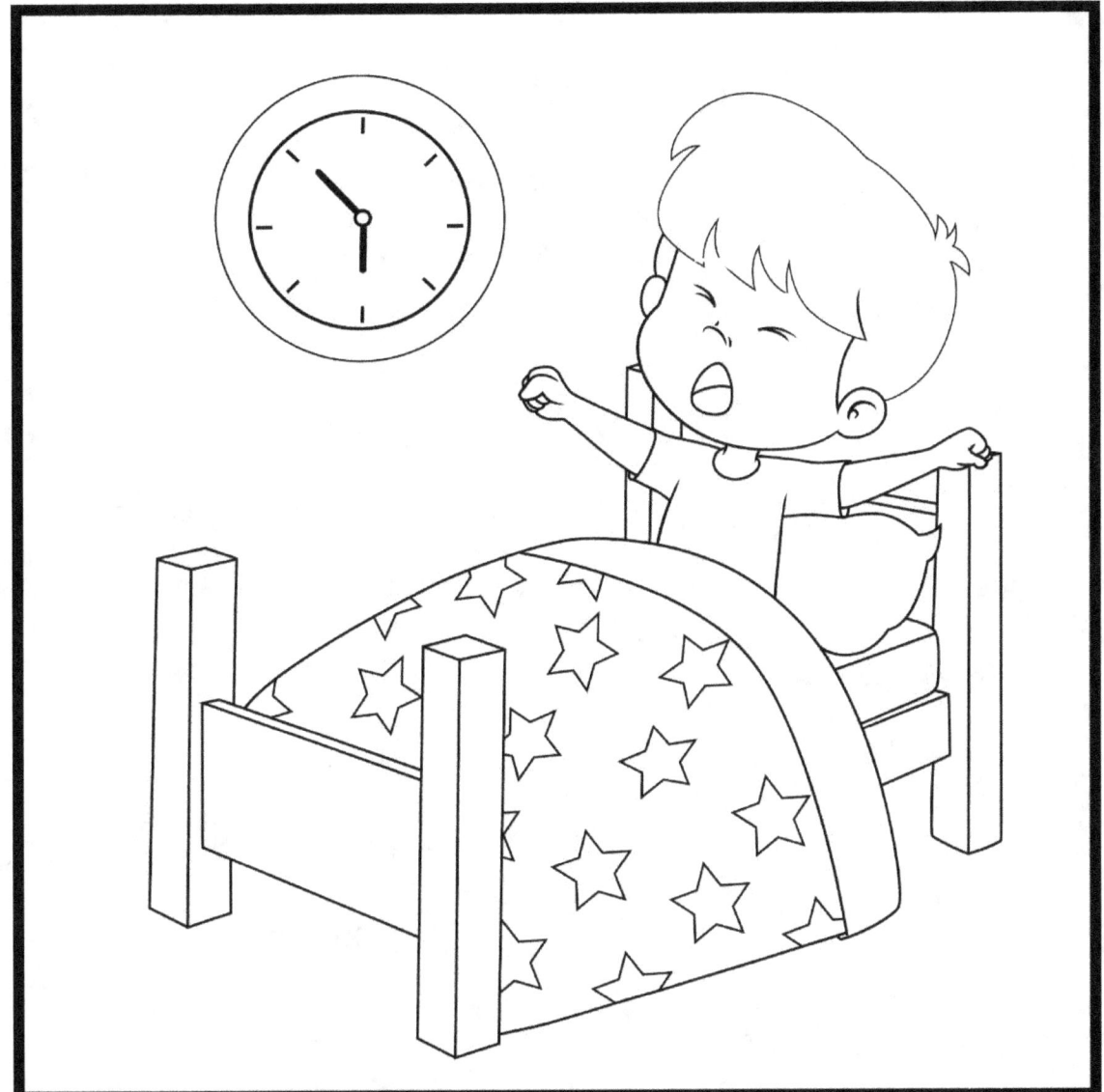

note:

_____

_____

_____

# OCTOBER 18TH

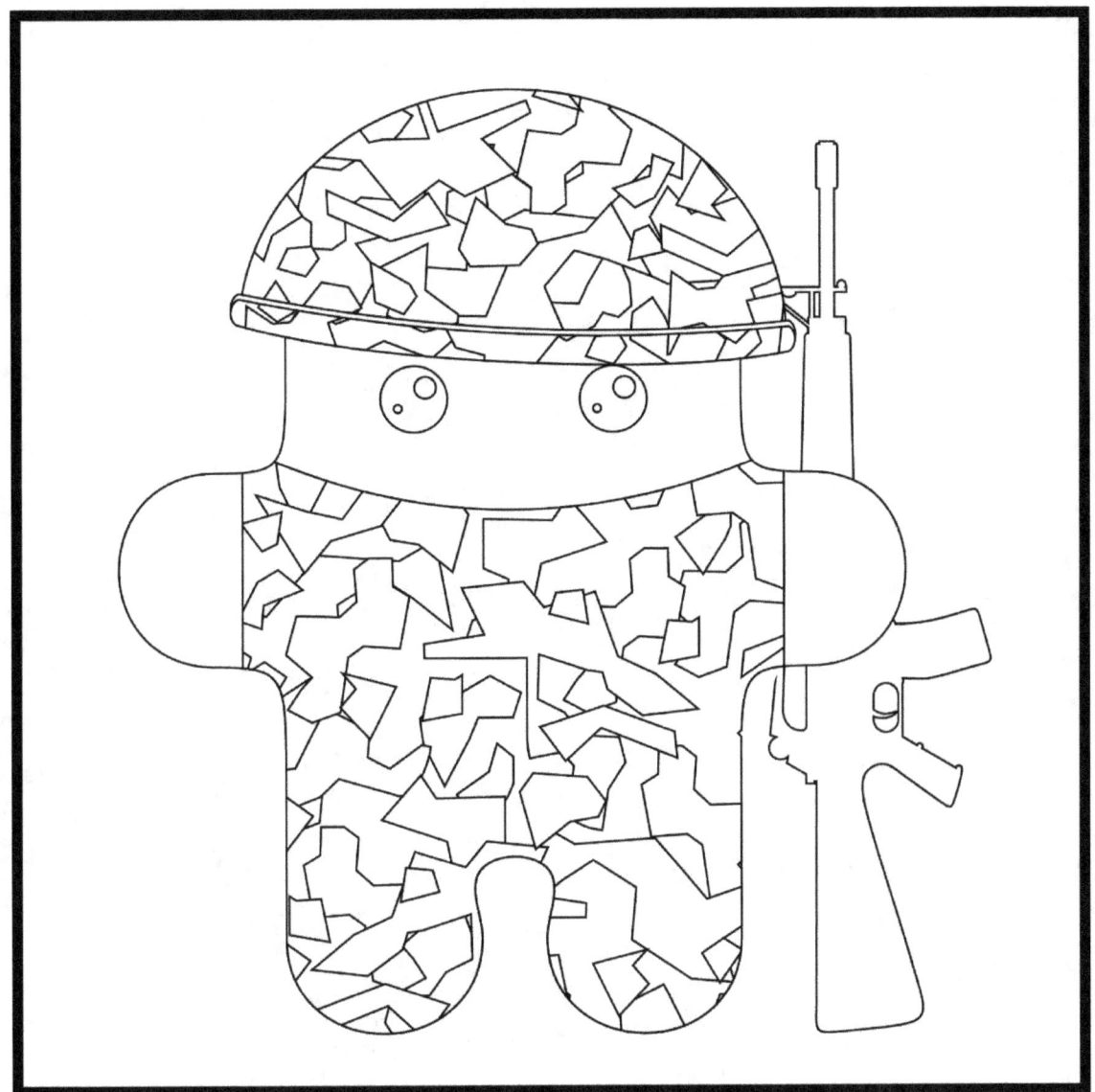

note:

_____

_____

_____

# OCTOBER 19TH

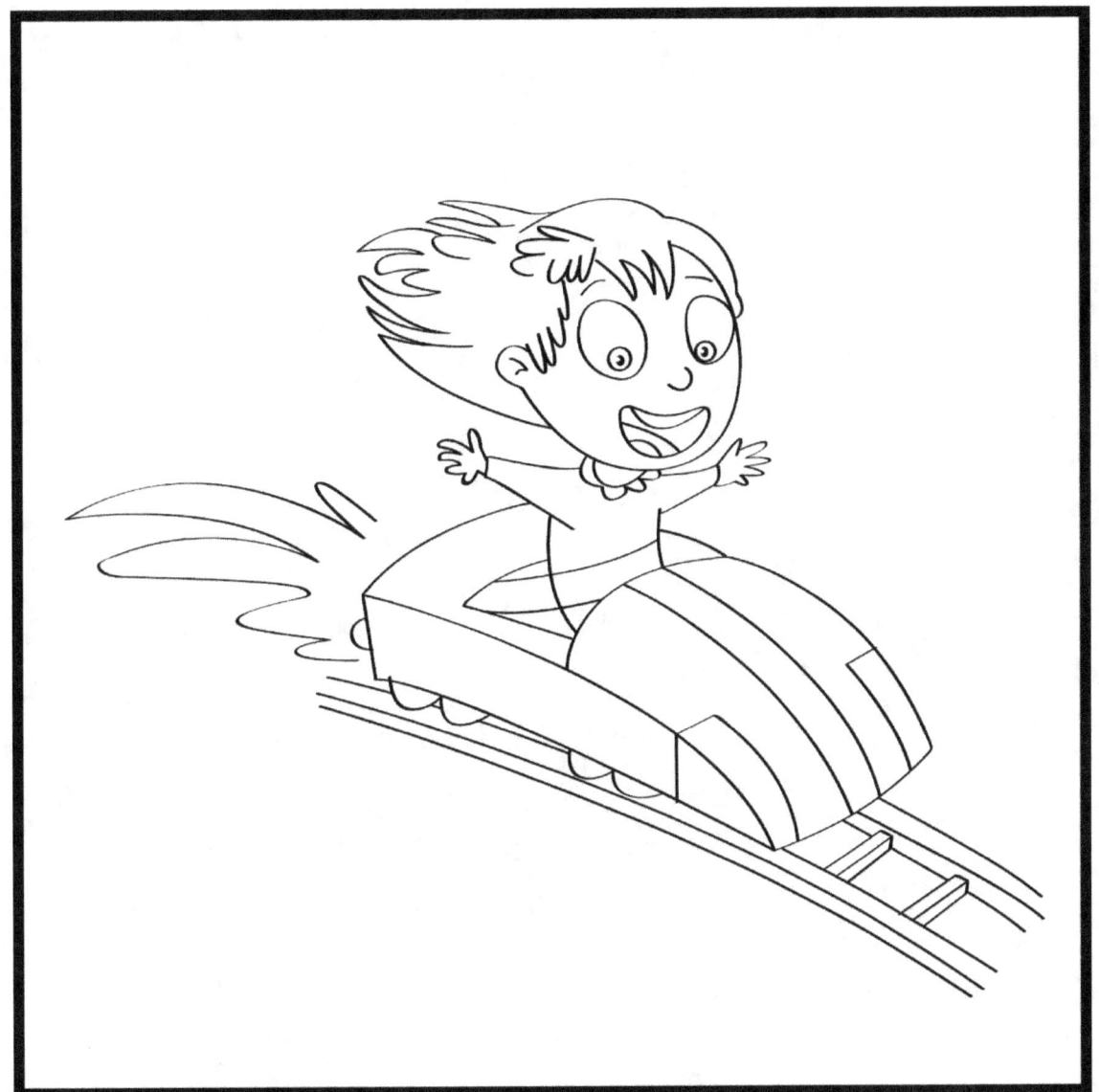

note:

_____

_____

_____

# OCTOBER 20TH

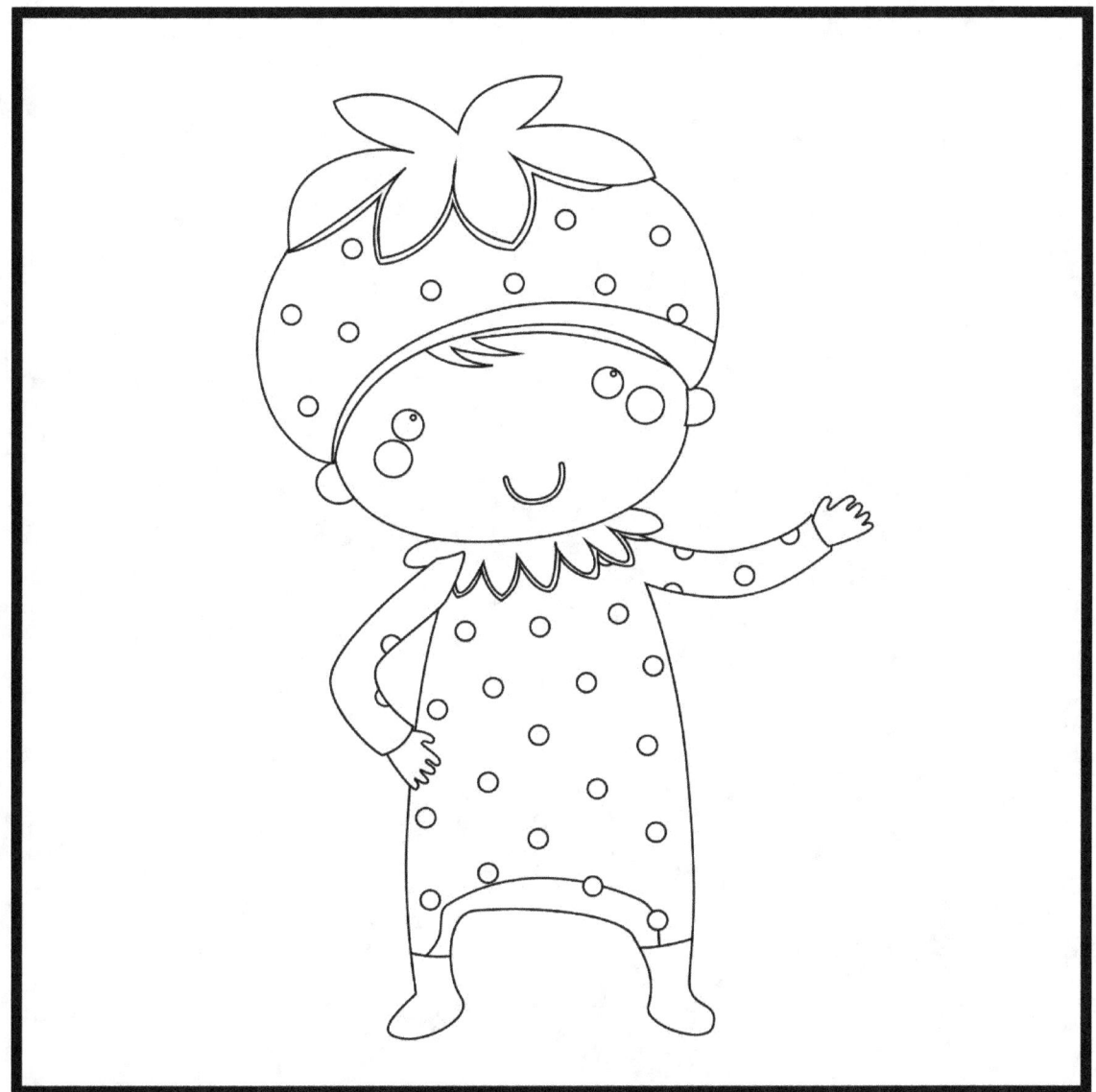

note:

_____

_____

_____

# OCTOBER 21TH

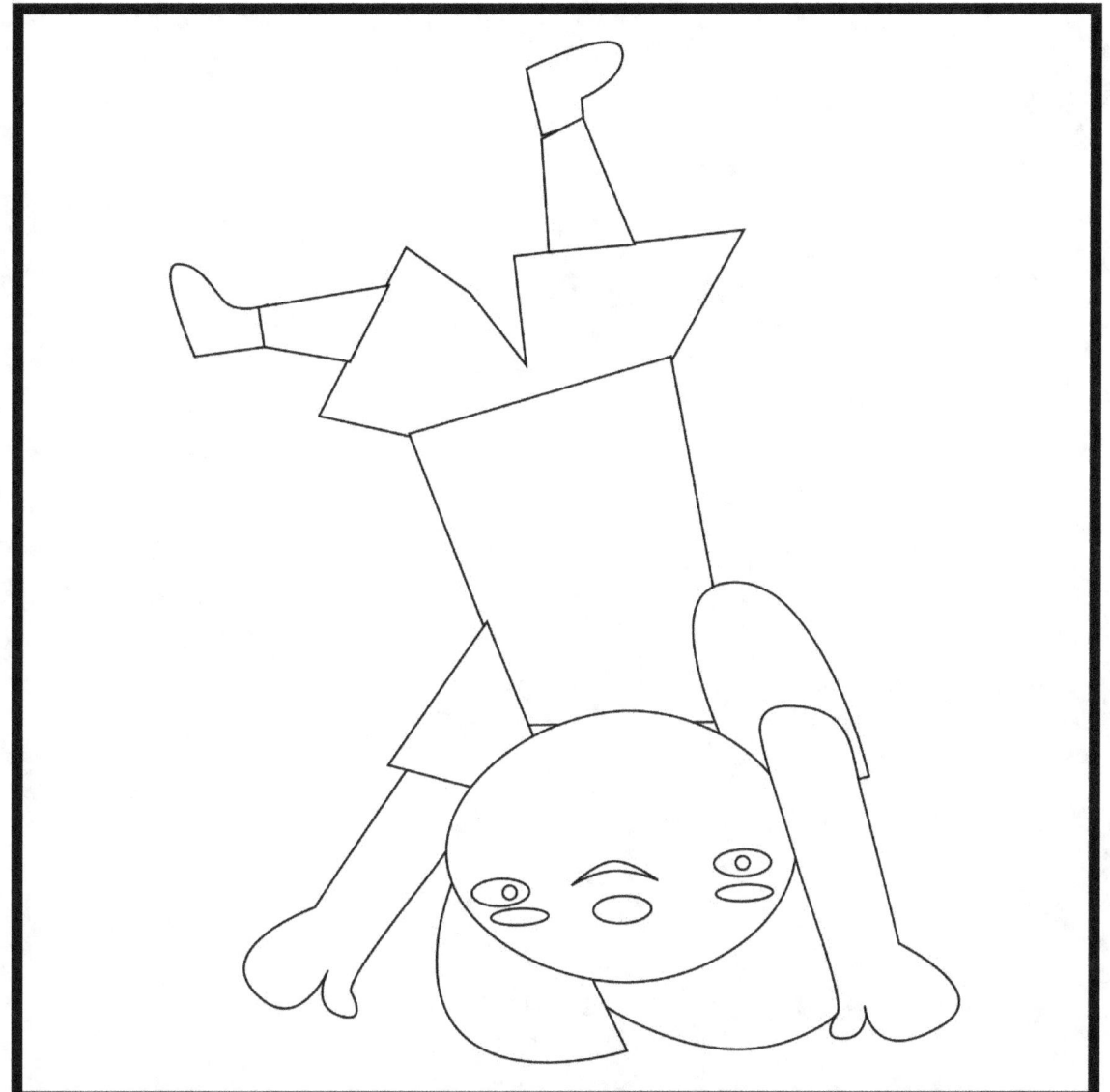

note:

_____

_____

_____

# OCTOBER 22TH

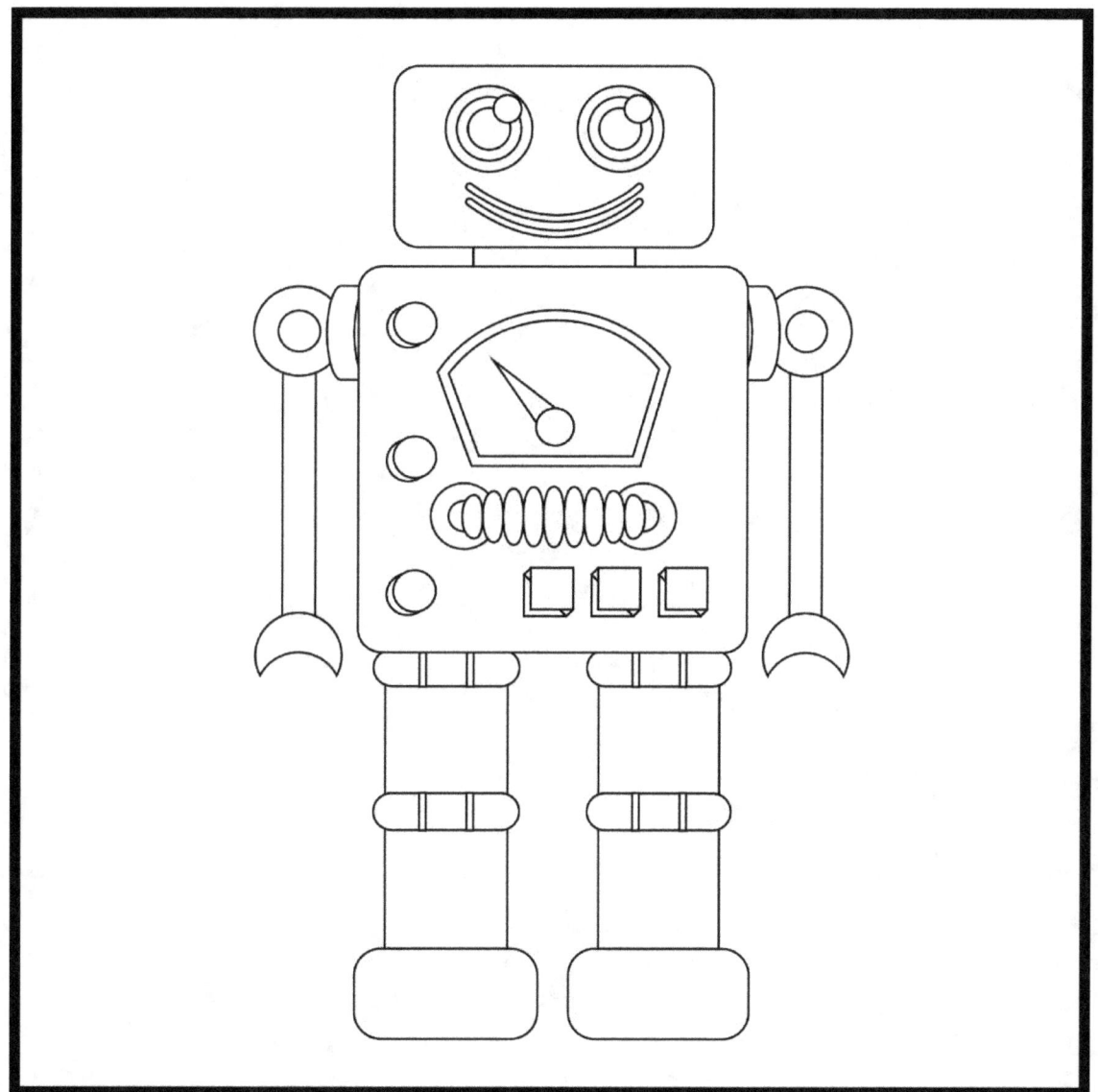

note:

_____

_____

_____

# OCTOBER 23TH

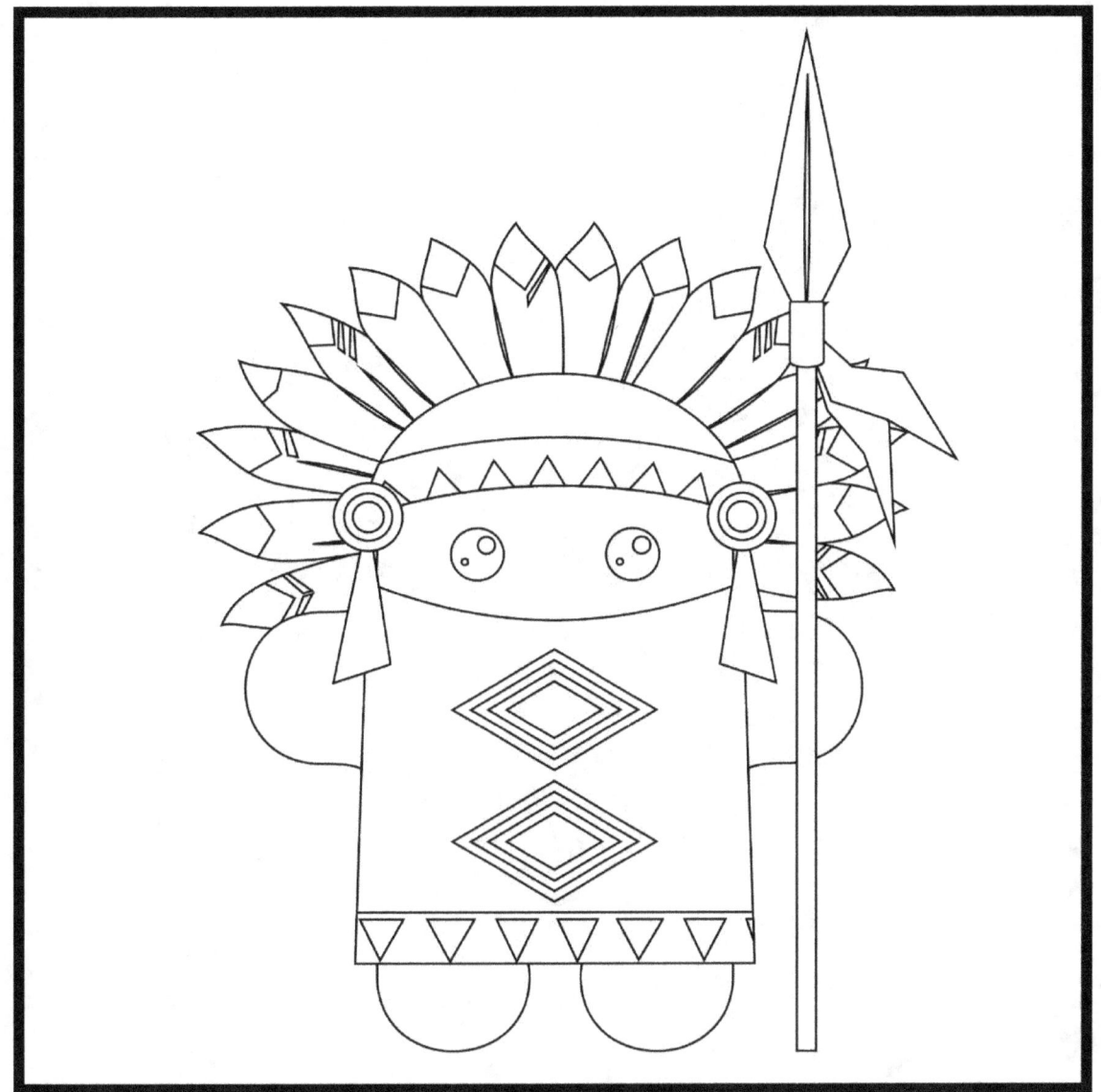

note:

_____

_____

_____

# OCTOBER 24TH

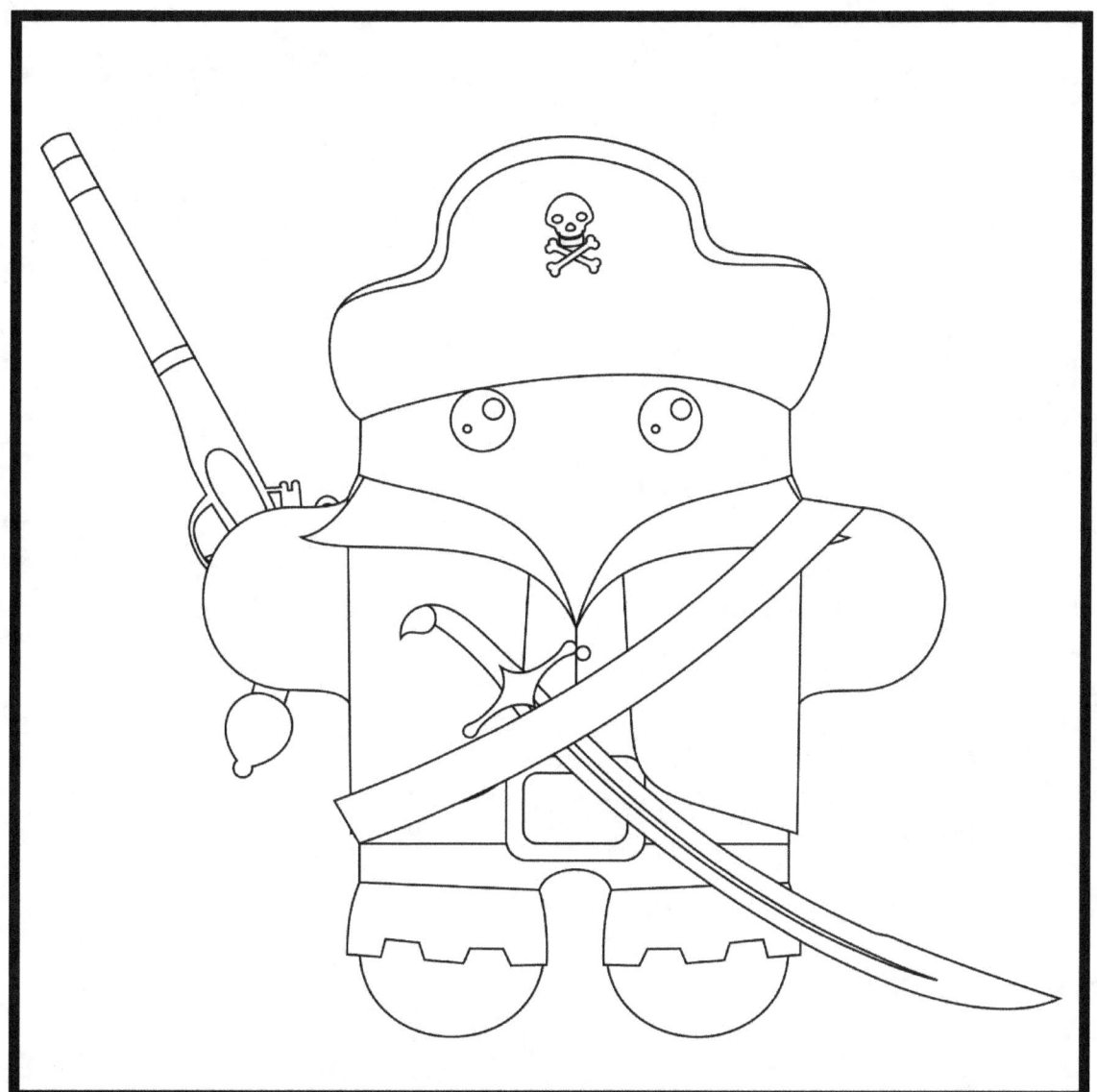

note:

_____

_____

_____

# OCTOBER 25TH

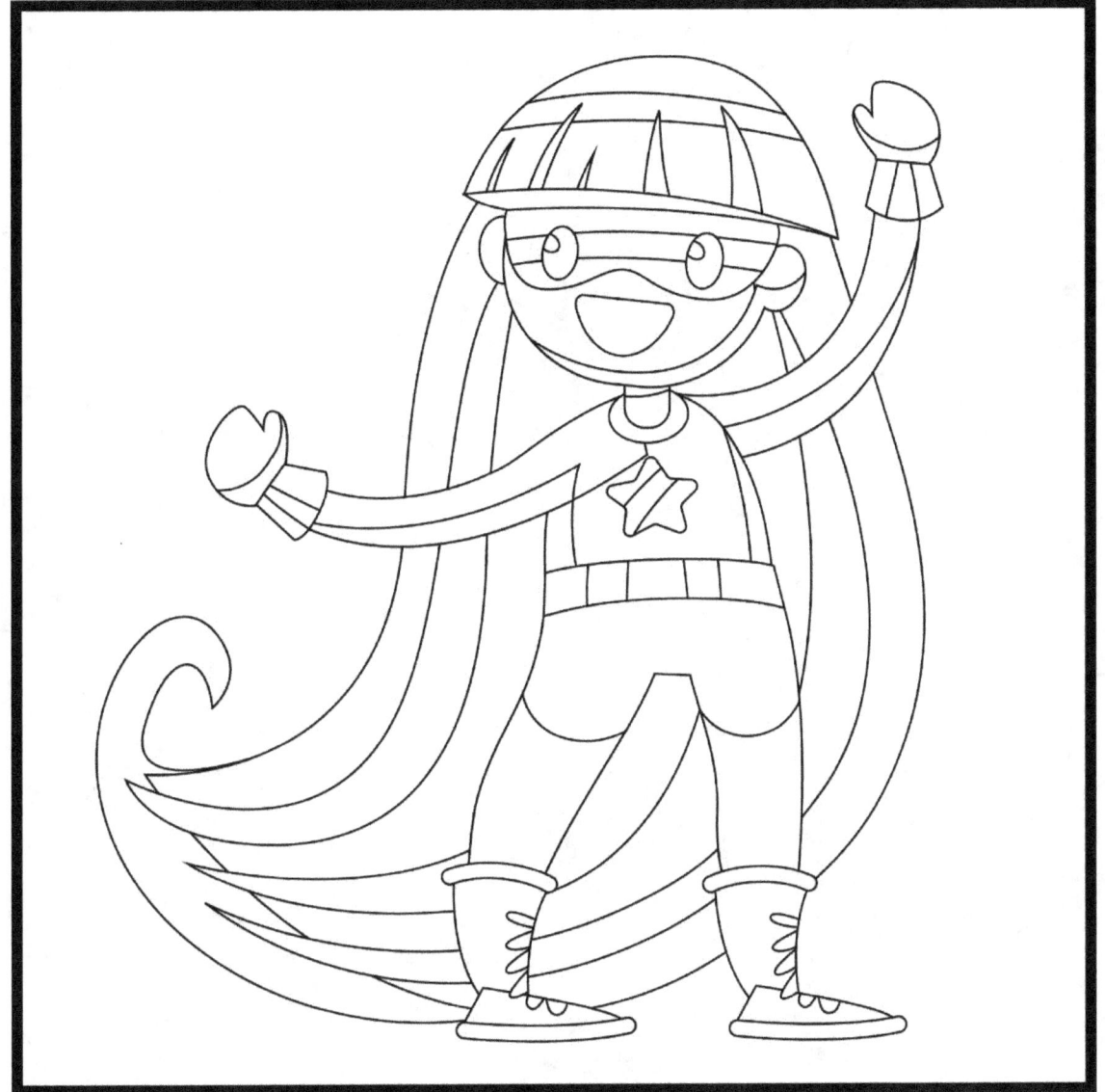

note:

_____

_____

_____

# OCTOBER 26TH

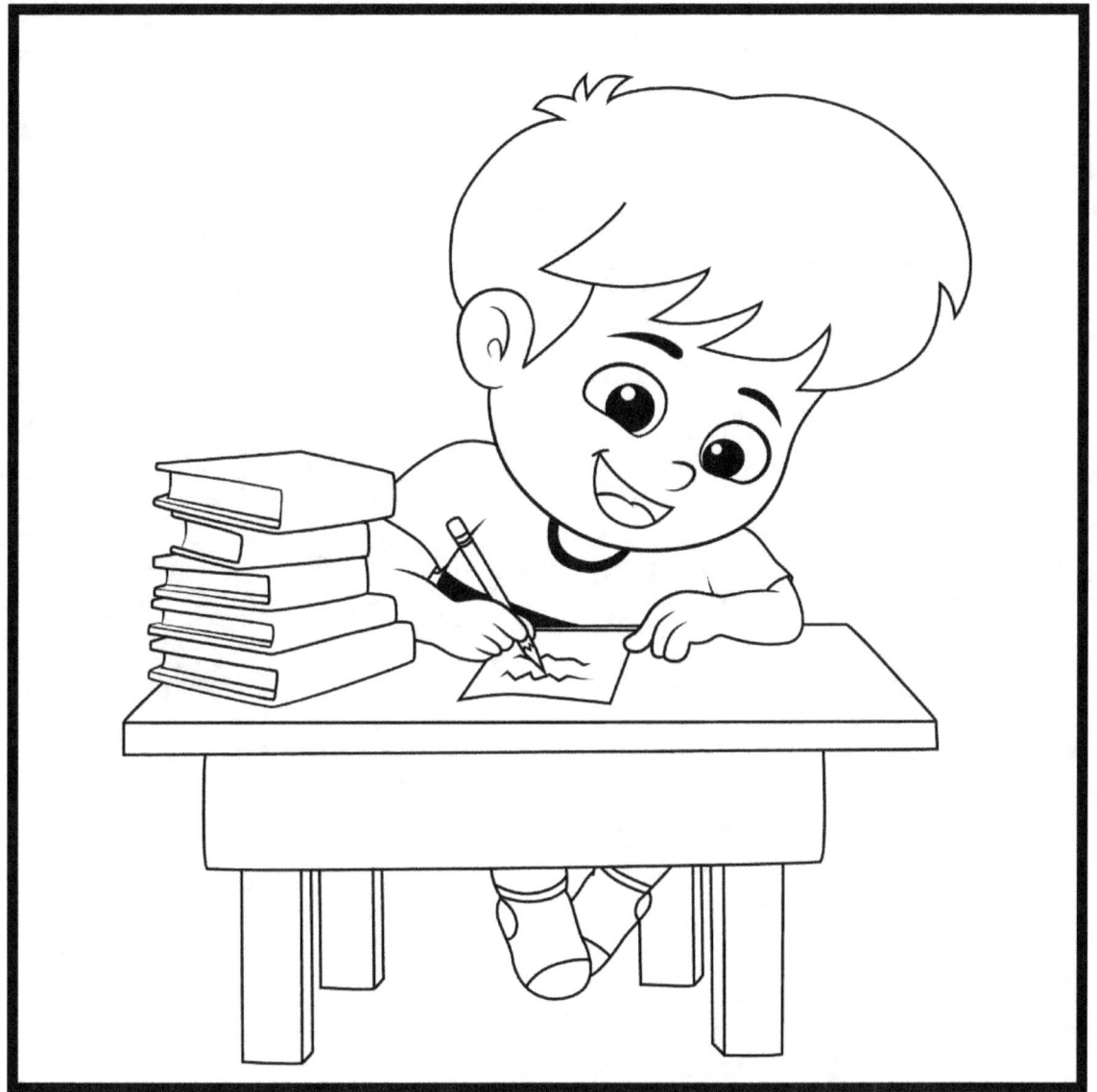

note:

_____

_____

_____

# OCTOBER 27TH

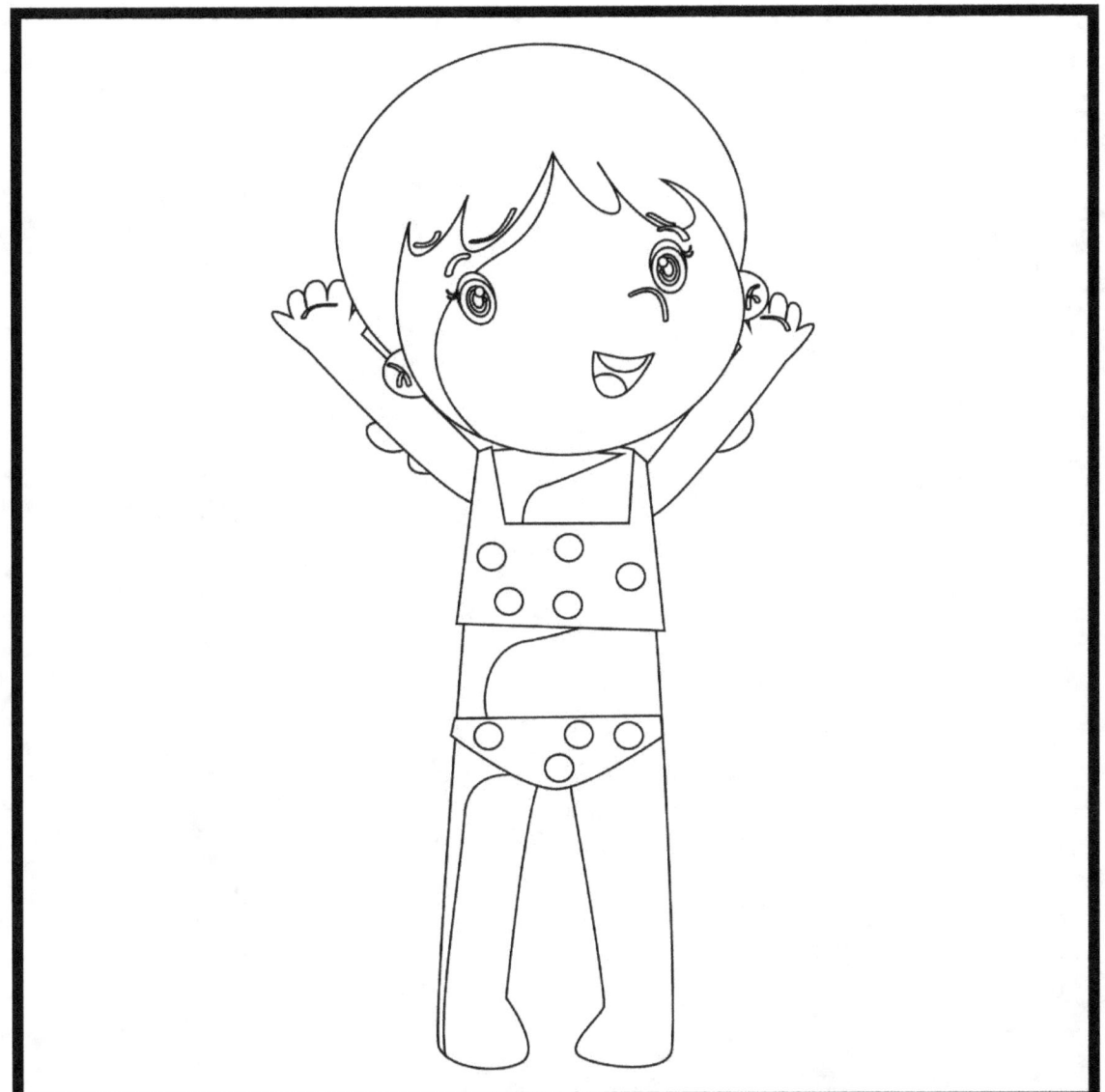

note:

_____

_____

_____

# OCTOBER 28TH

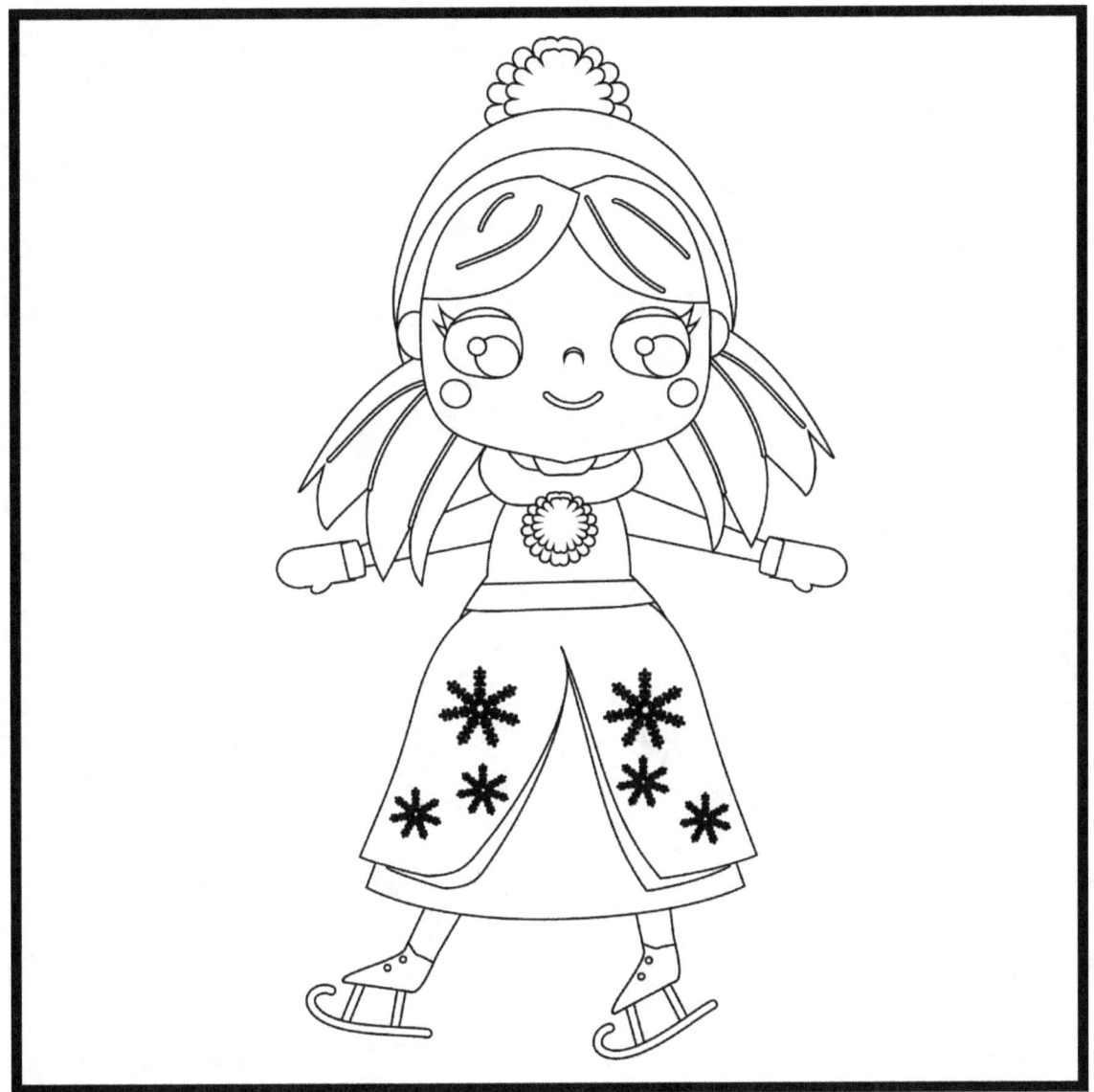

note:

_____

_____

_____

# OCTOBER 29TH

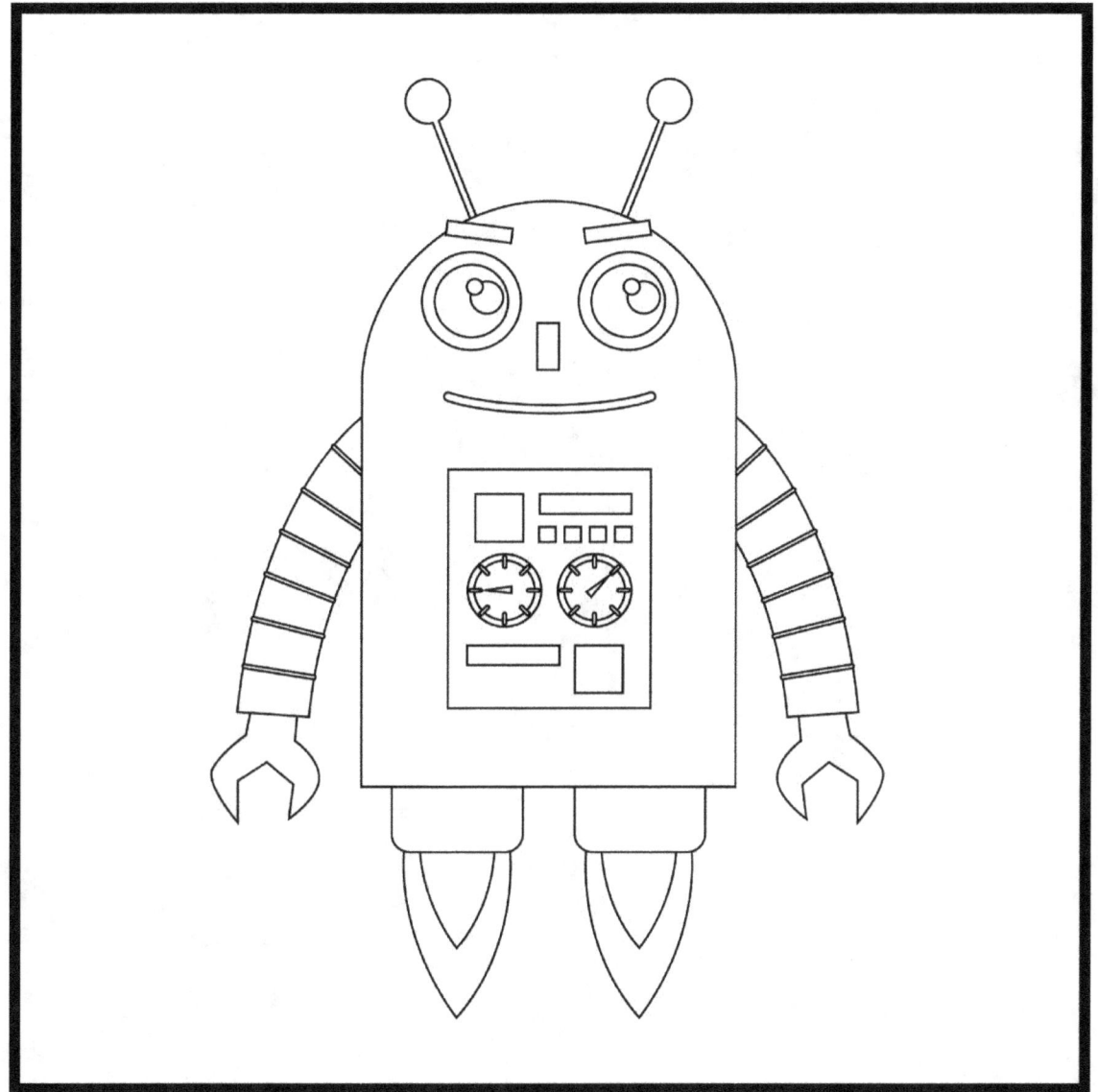

note:

_____

_____

_____

# OCTOBER 30TH

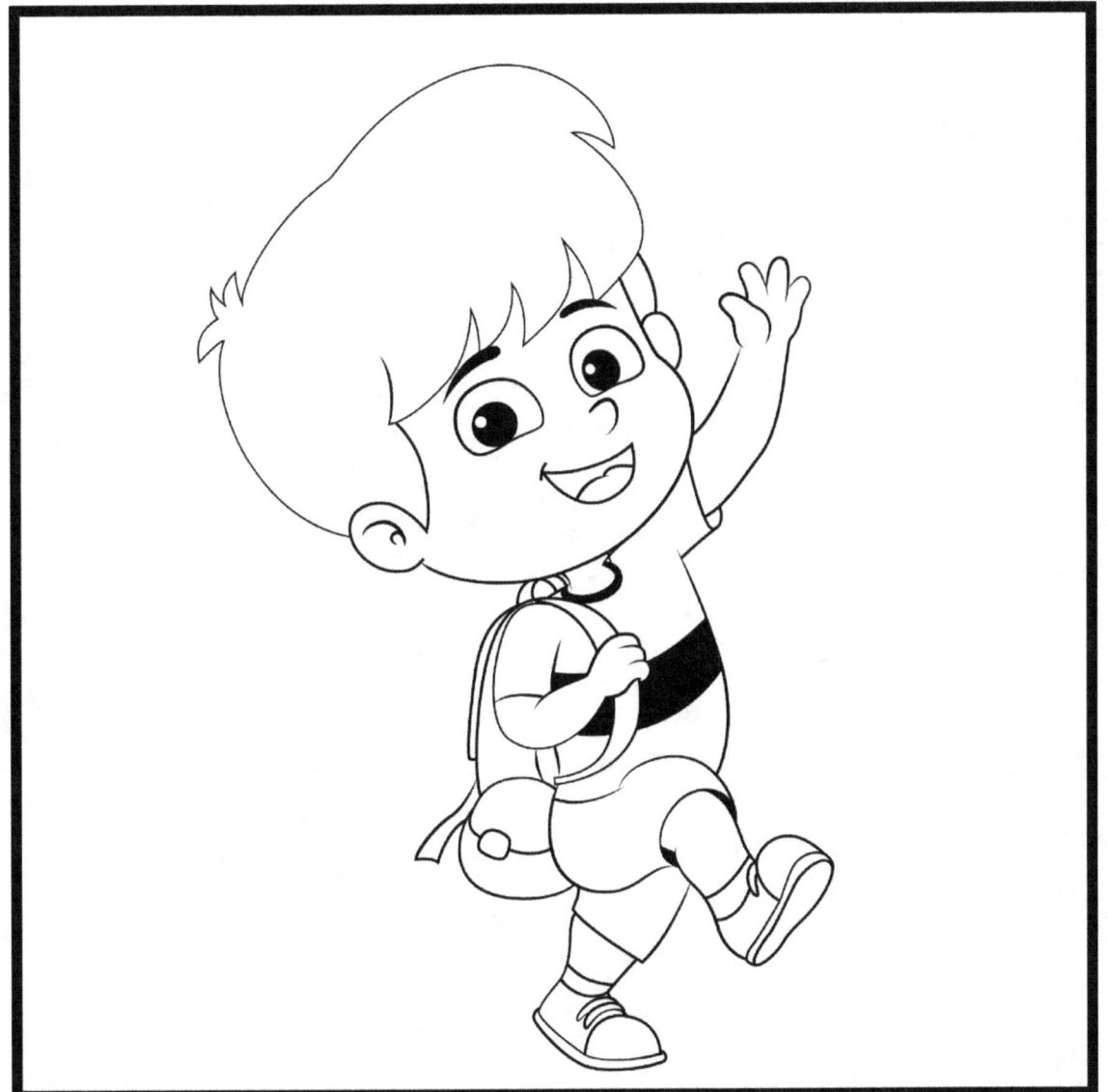

note:

_____

_____

_____

# OCTOBER 3ITH

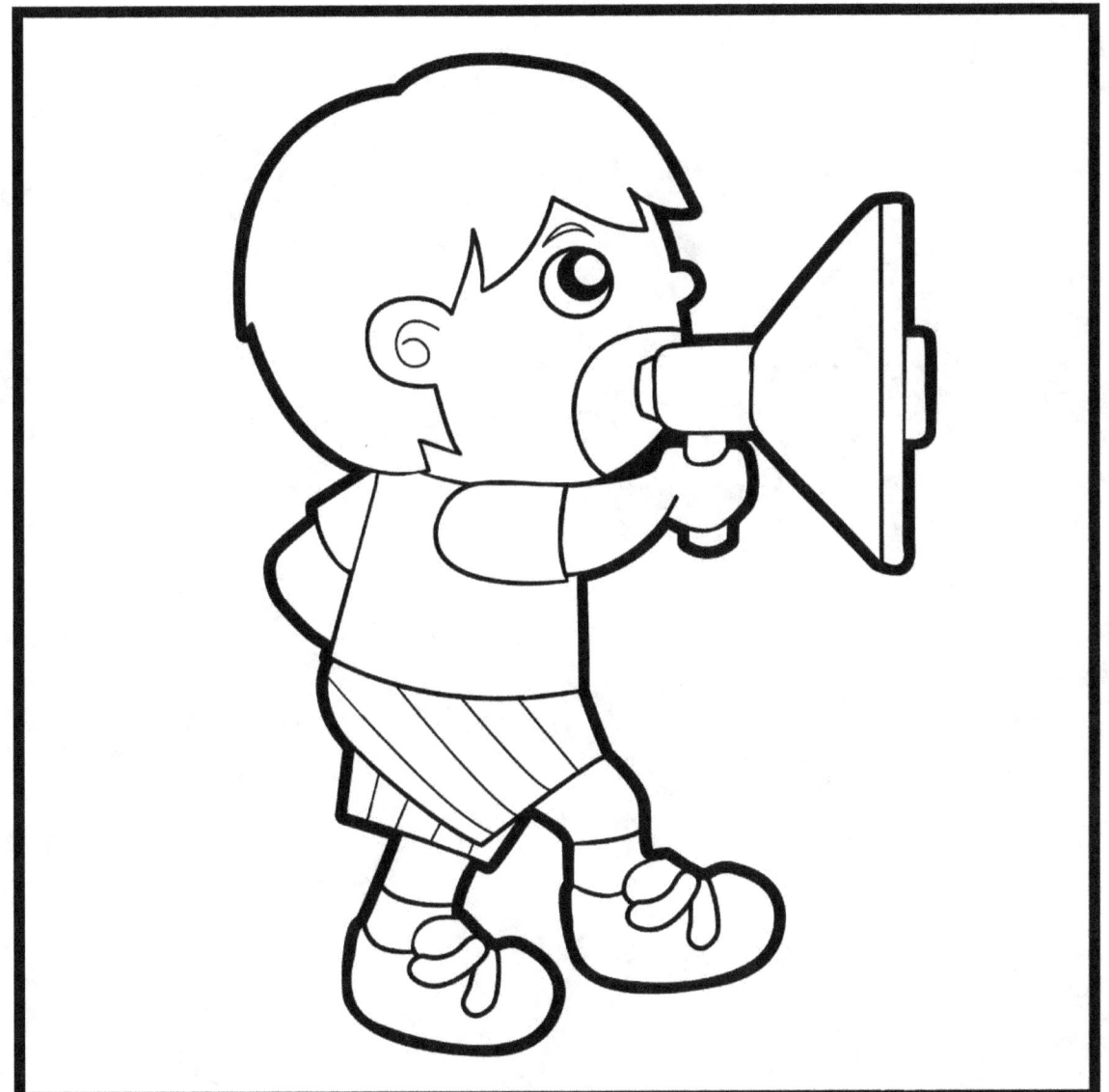

note:

_____

_____

_____

# OCTOBER 32TH

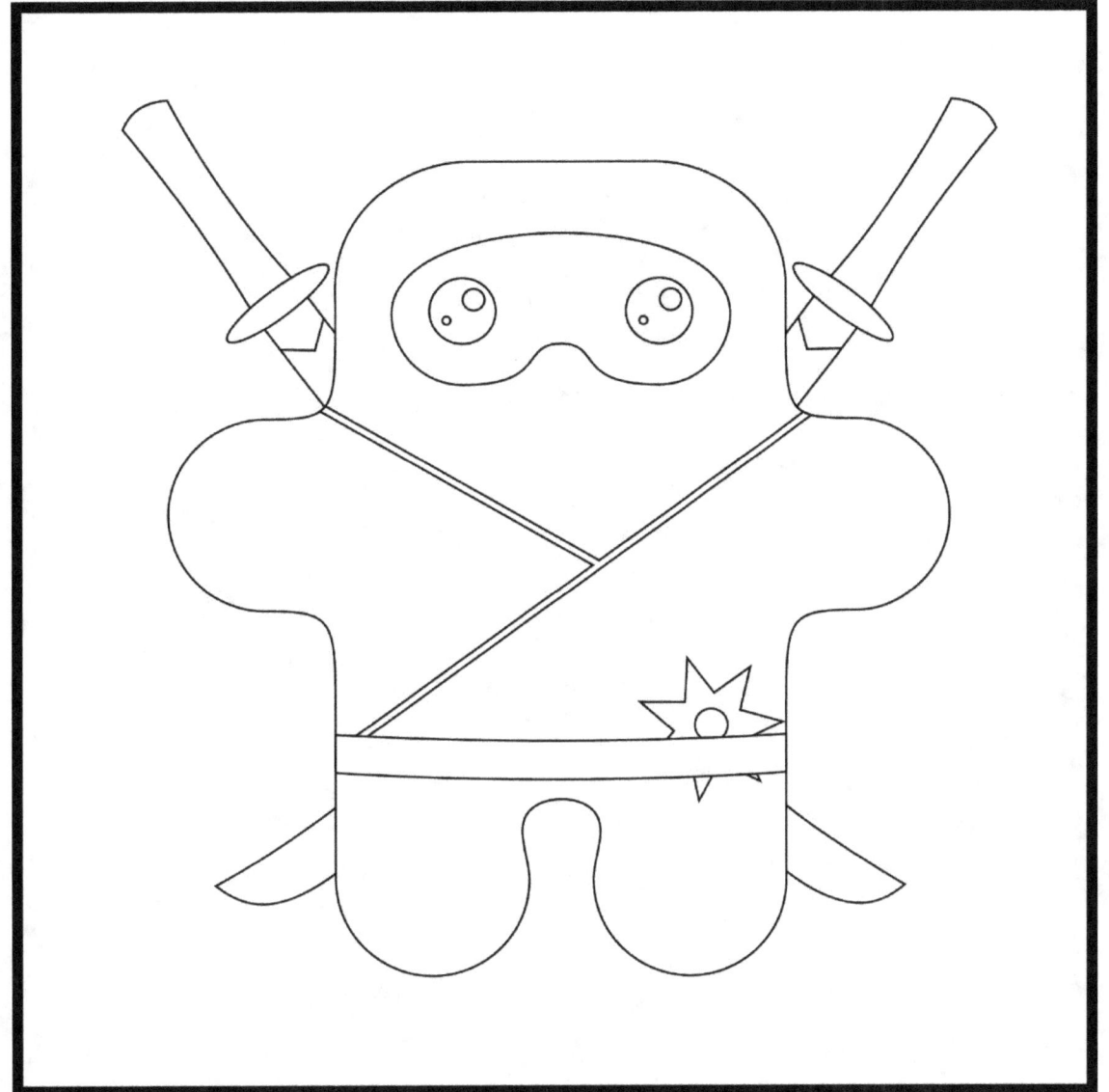

note:

_____

_____

_____

# OCTOBER 33TH

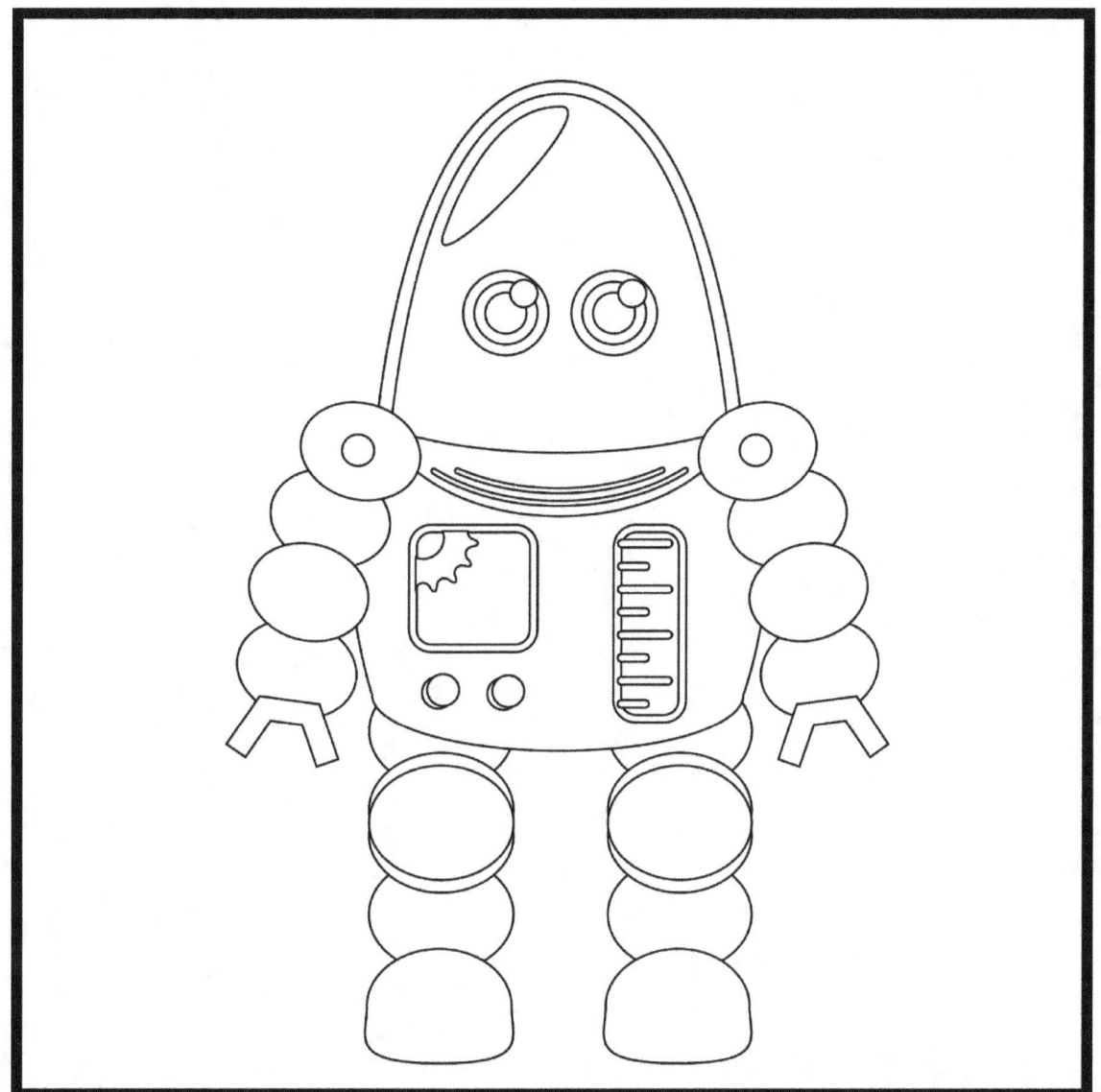

note:

_____

_____

_____

# OCTOBER 34TH

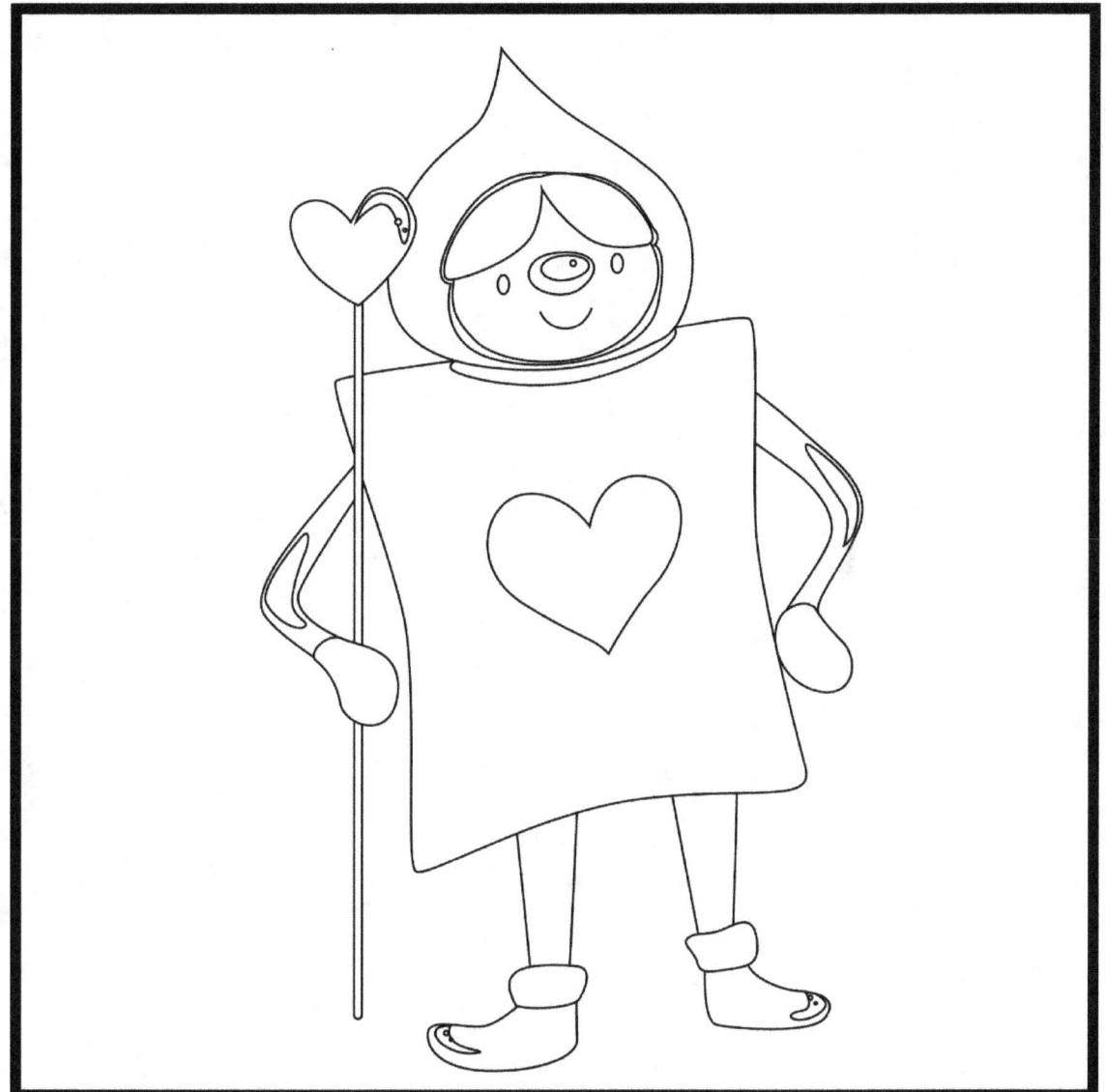

note:

_____

_____

_____

# OCTOBER 35TH

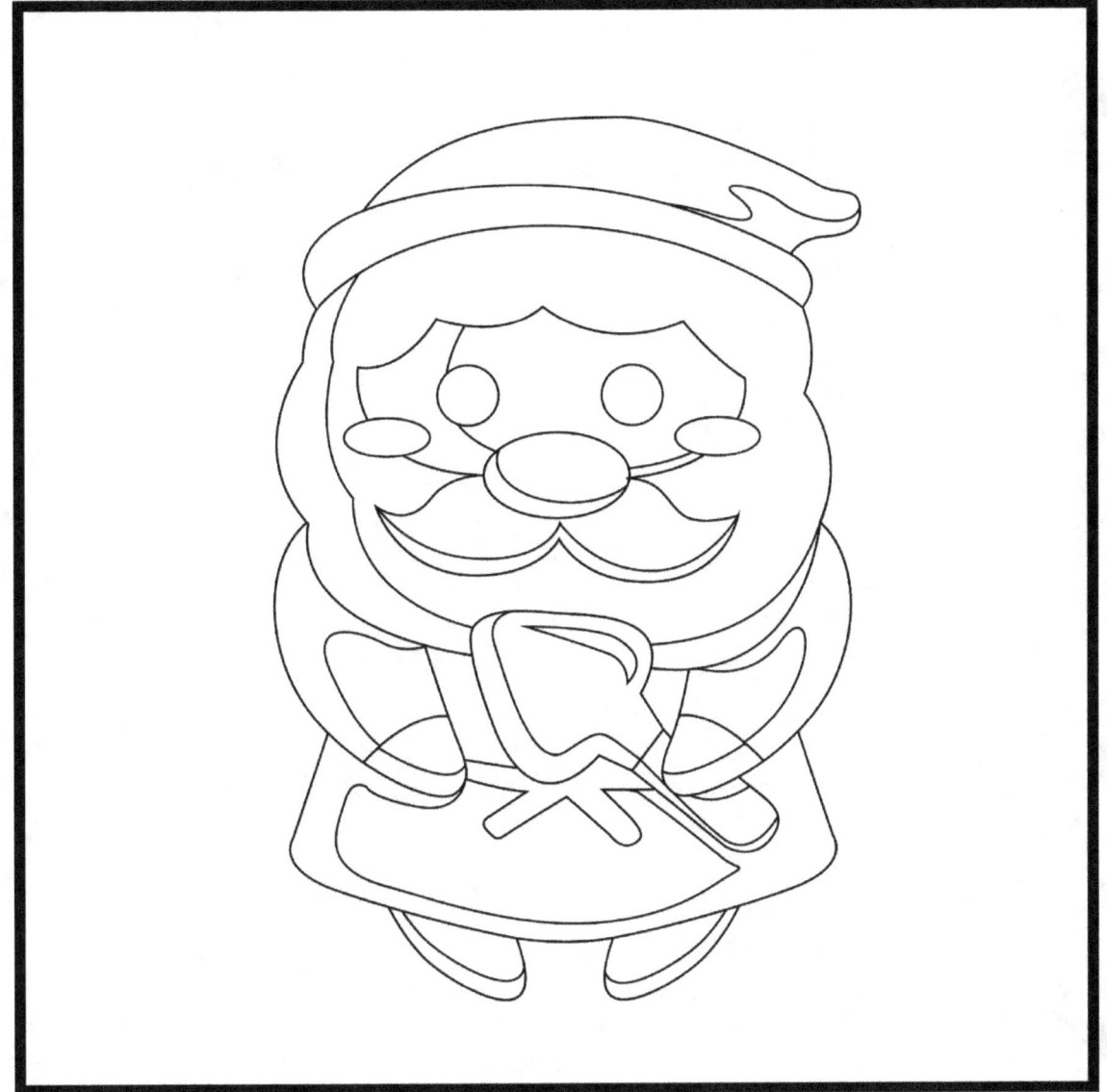

note:

_____

_____

_____

# OCTOBER 36TH

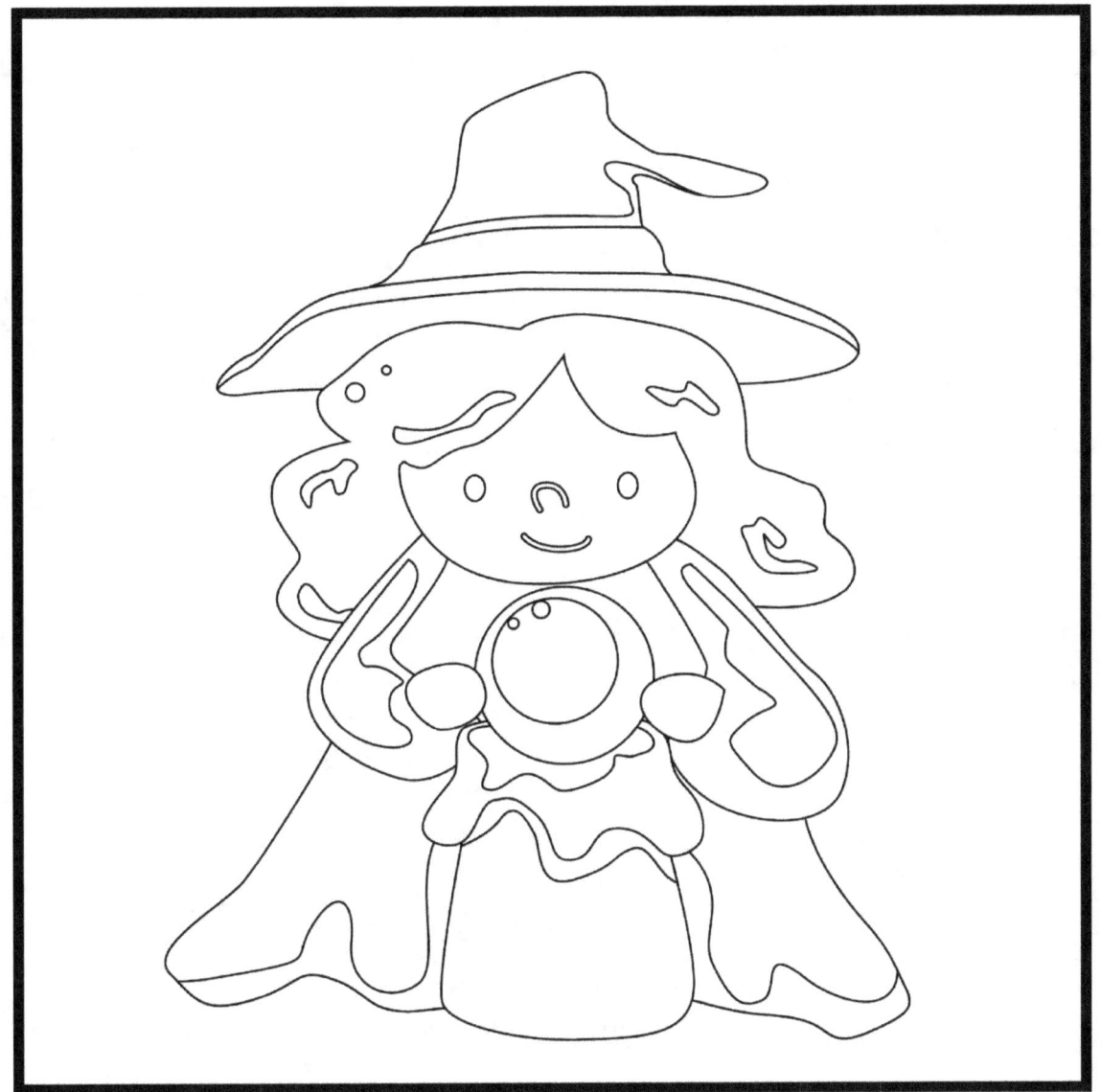

note:

_____

_____

_____

# OCTOBER 37TH

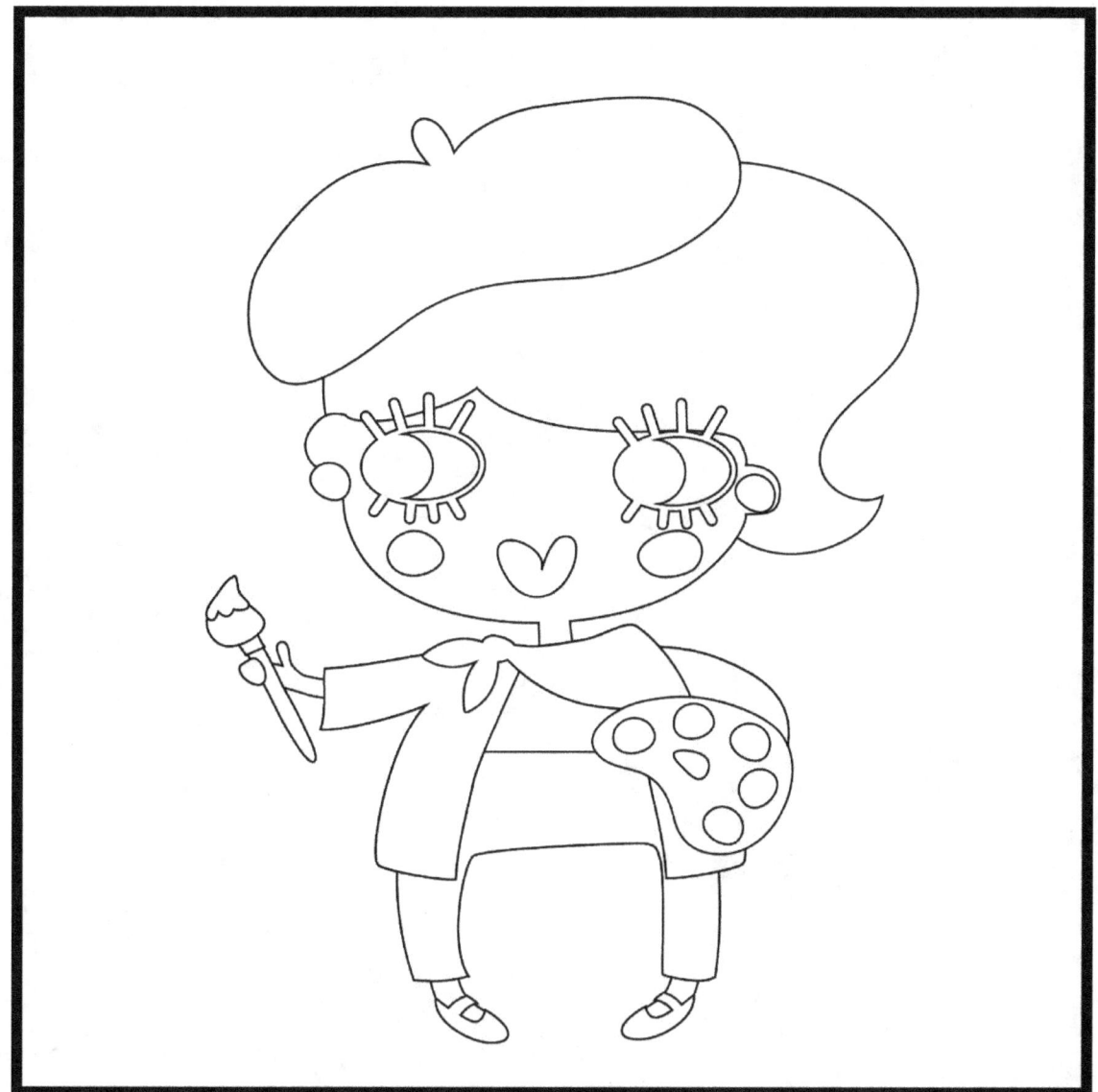

note:

_____

_____

_____

# OCTOBER 38TH

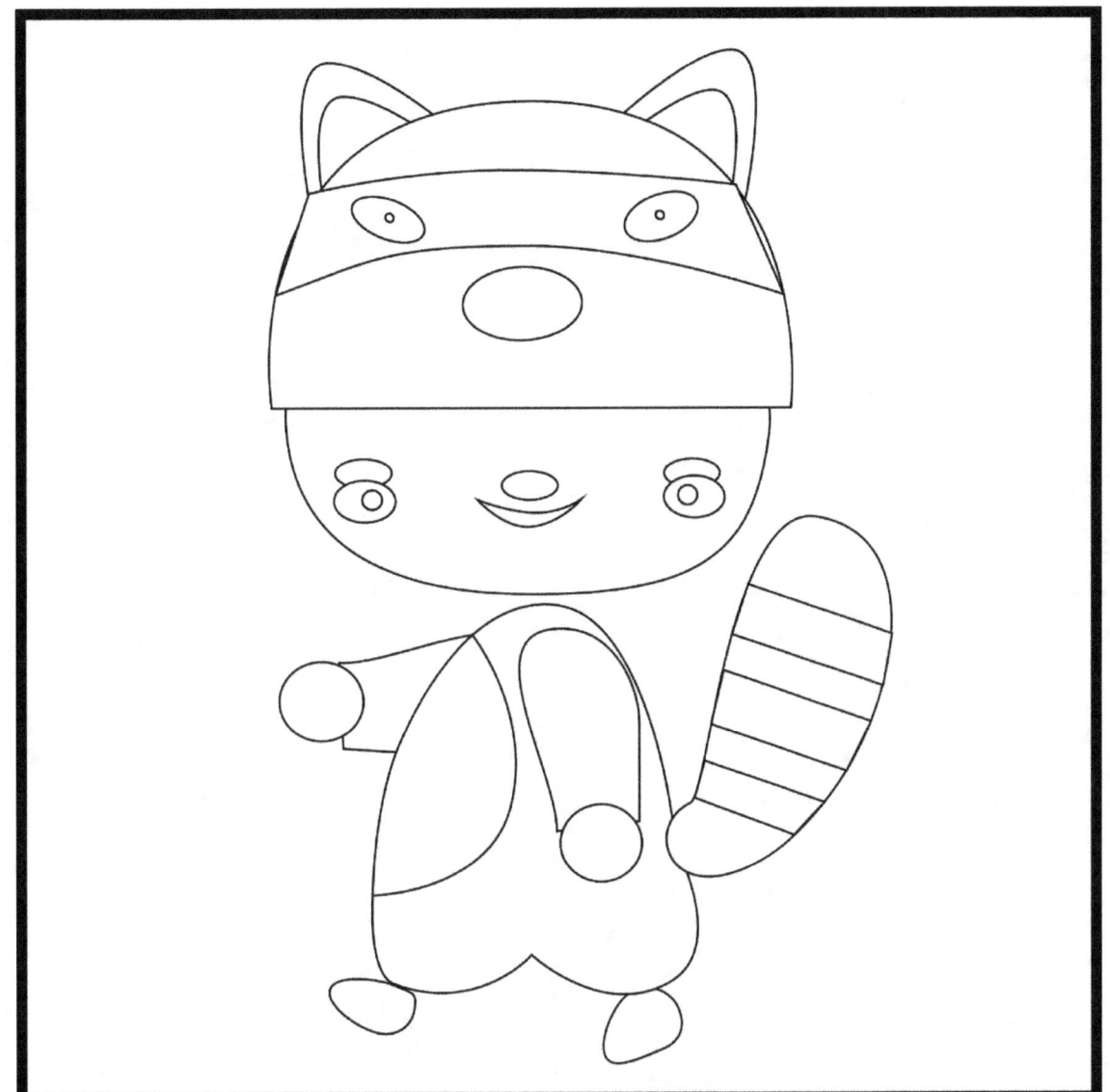

note:

_____

_____

_____

# OCTOBER 39TH

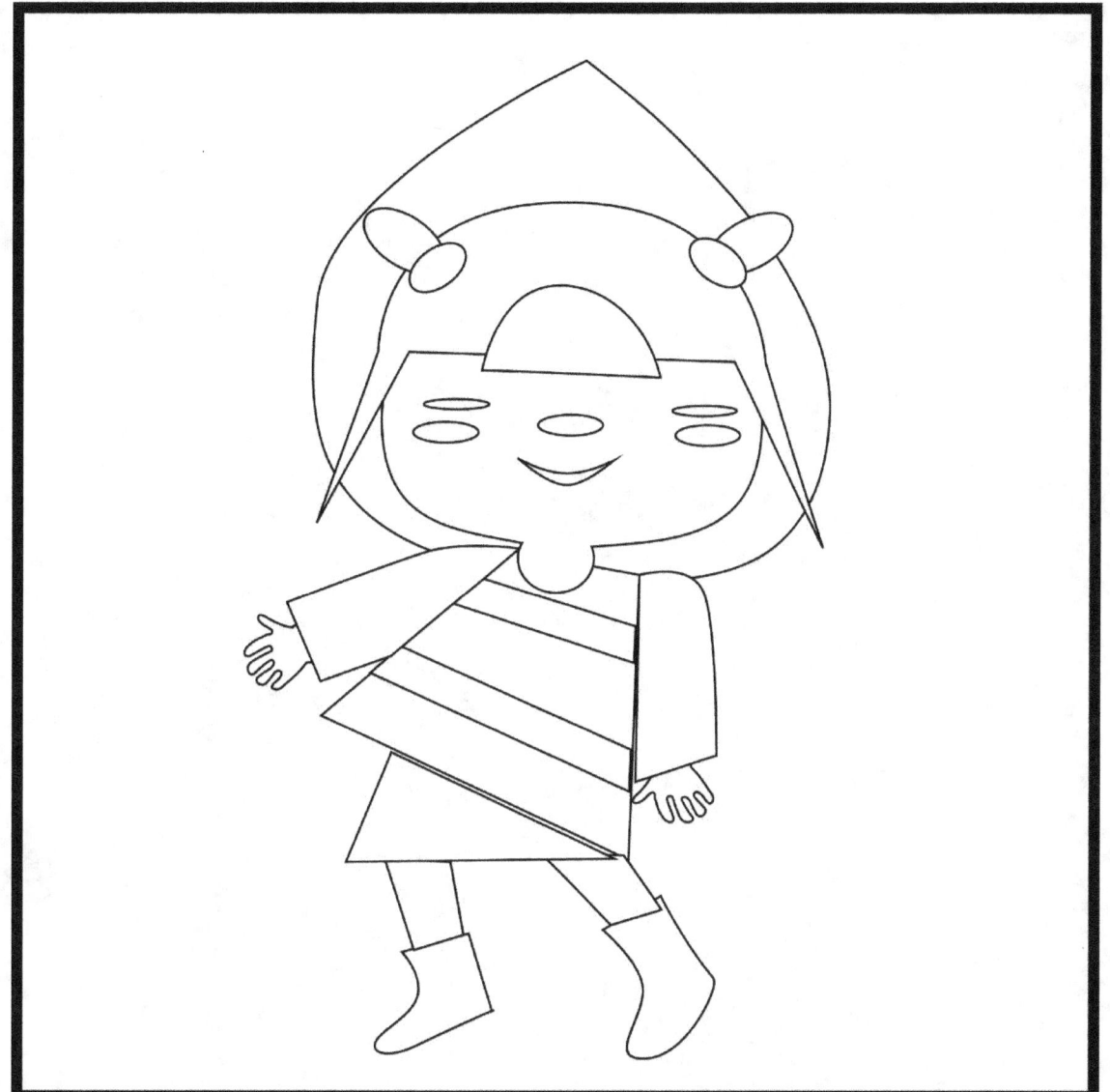

note:

_____

_____

_____

# OCTOBER 40TH

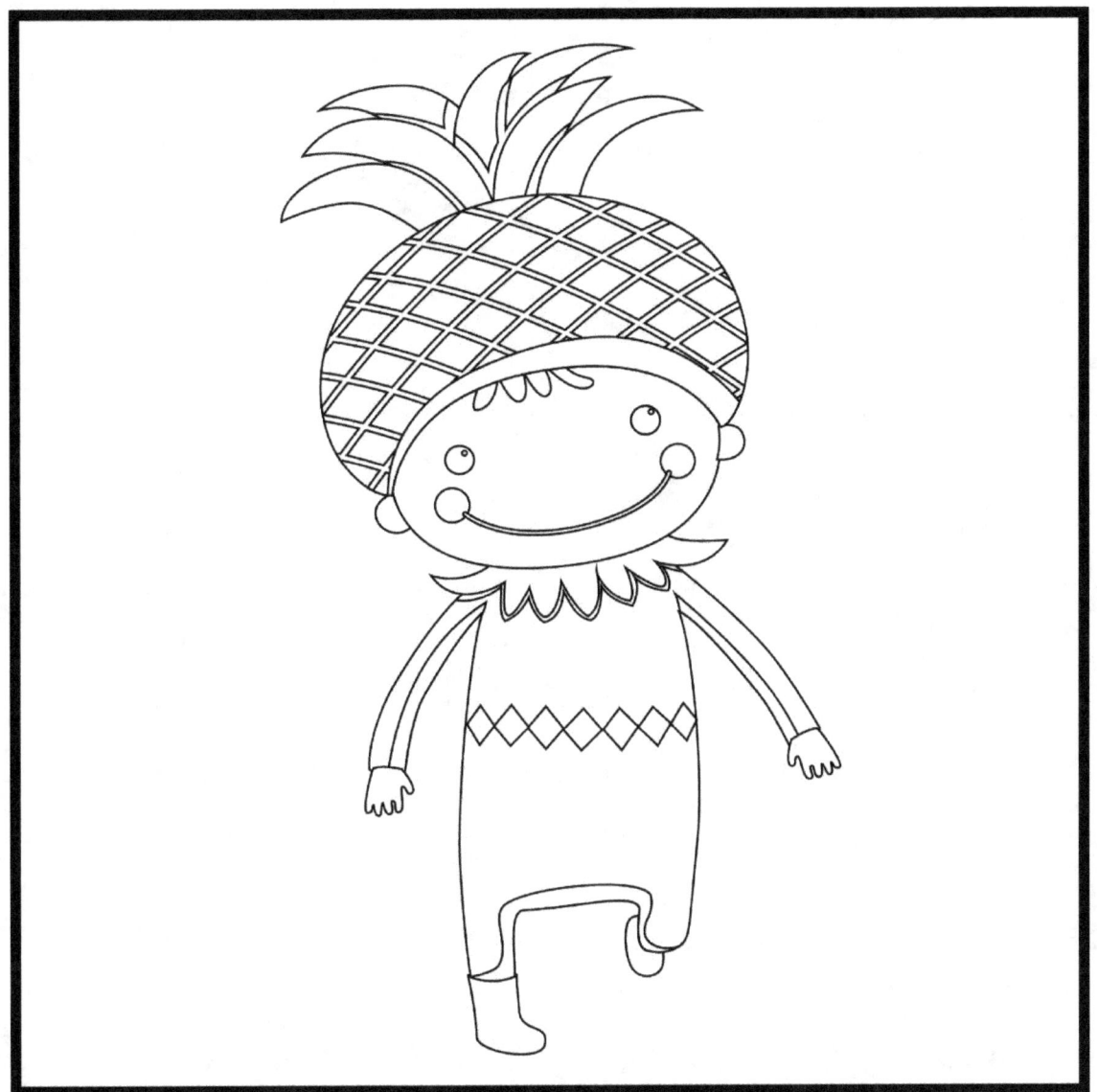

note:

_____

_____

_____

# OCTOBER 41TH

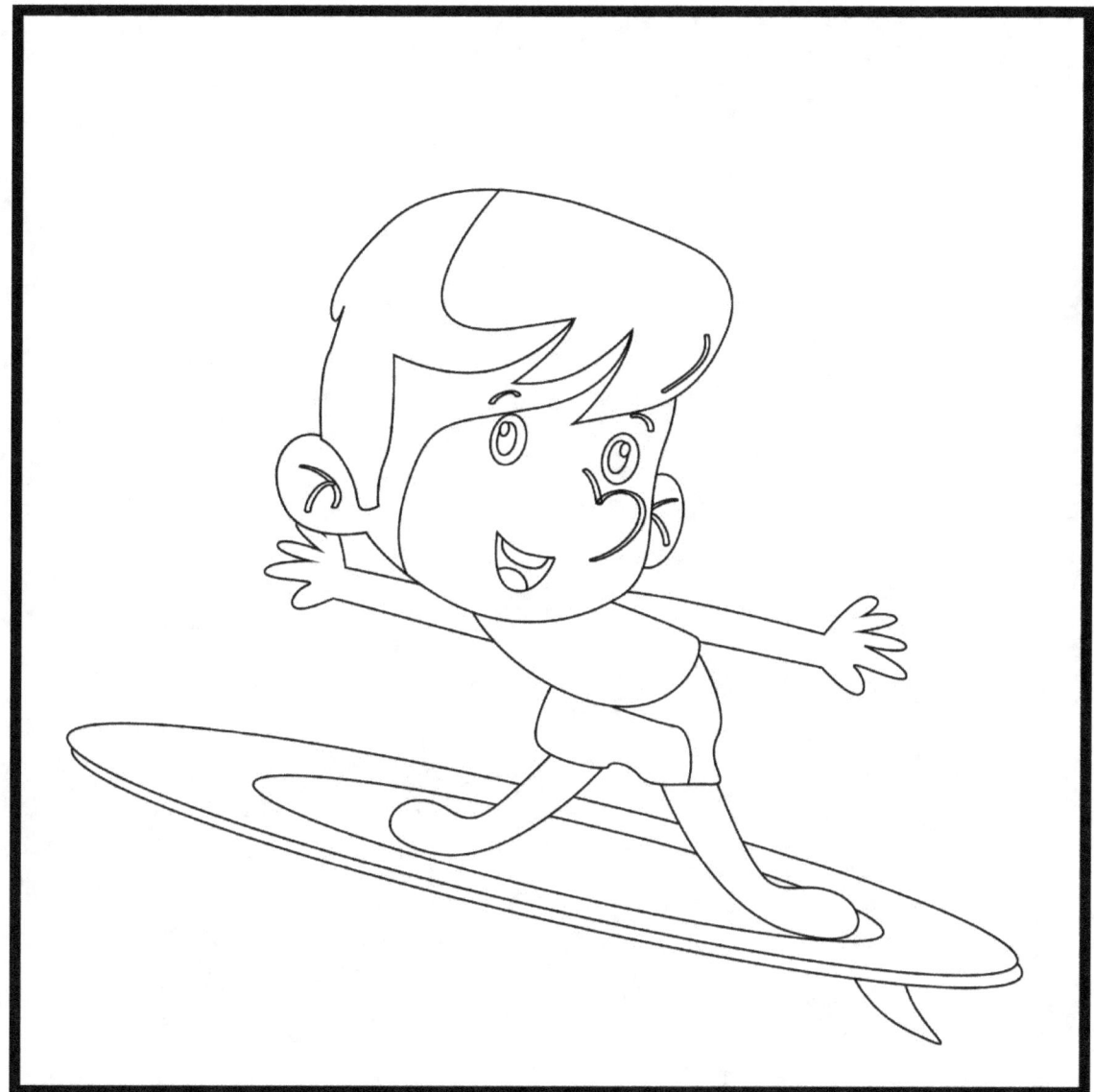

note:

_____

_____

_____

# OCTOBER 42TH

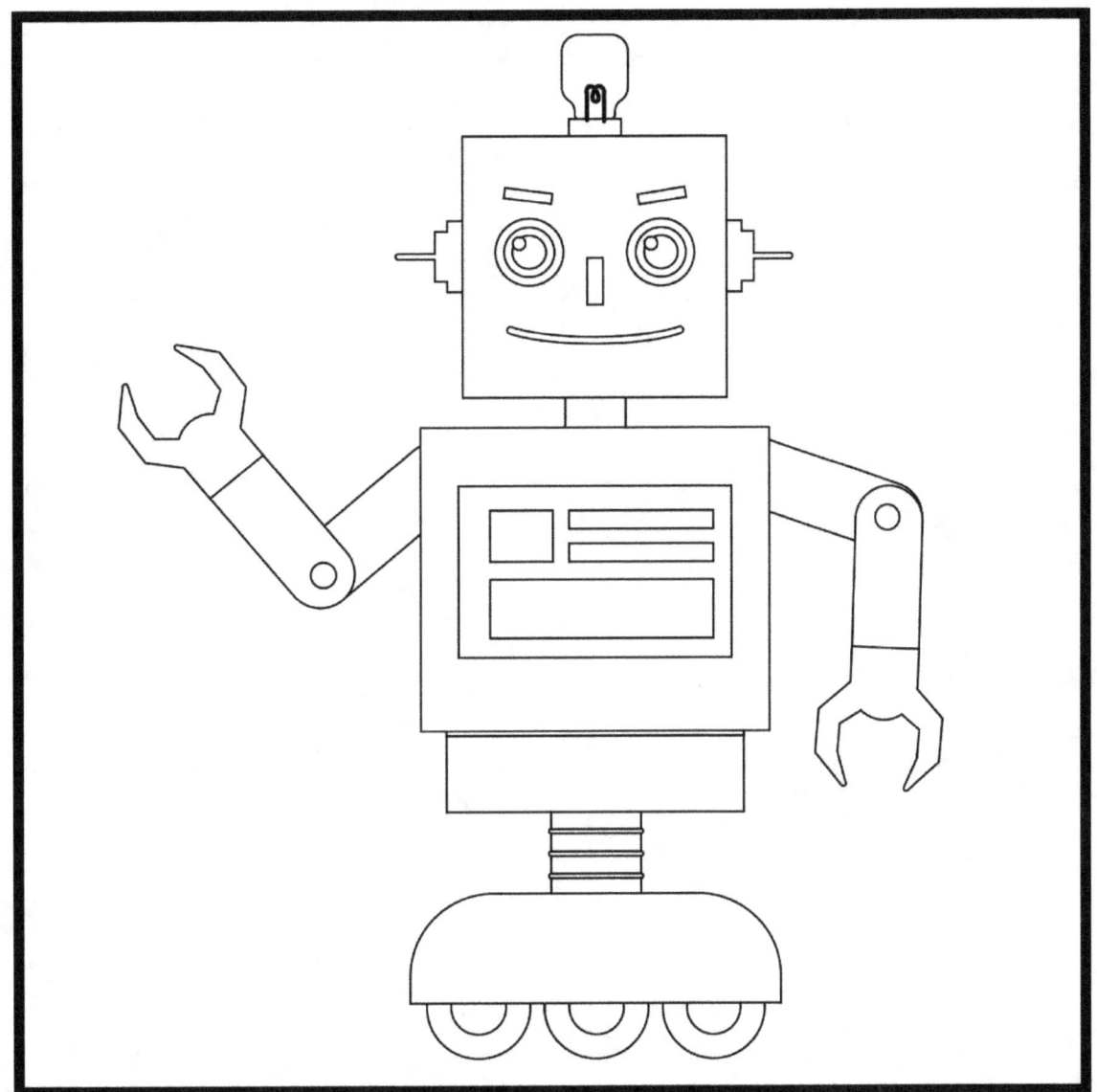

note:

_____

_____

_____

# OCTOBER 43TH

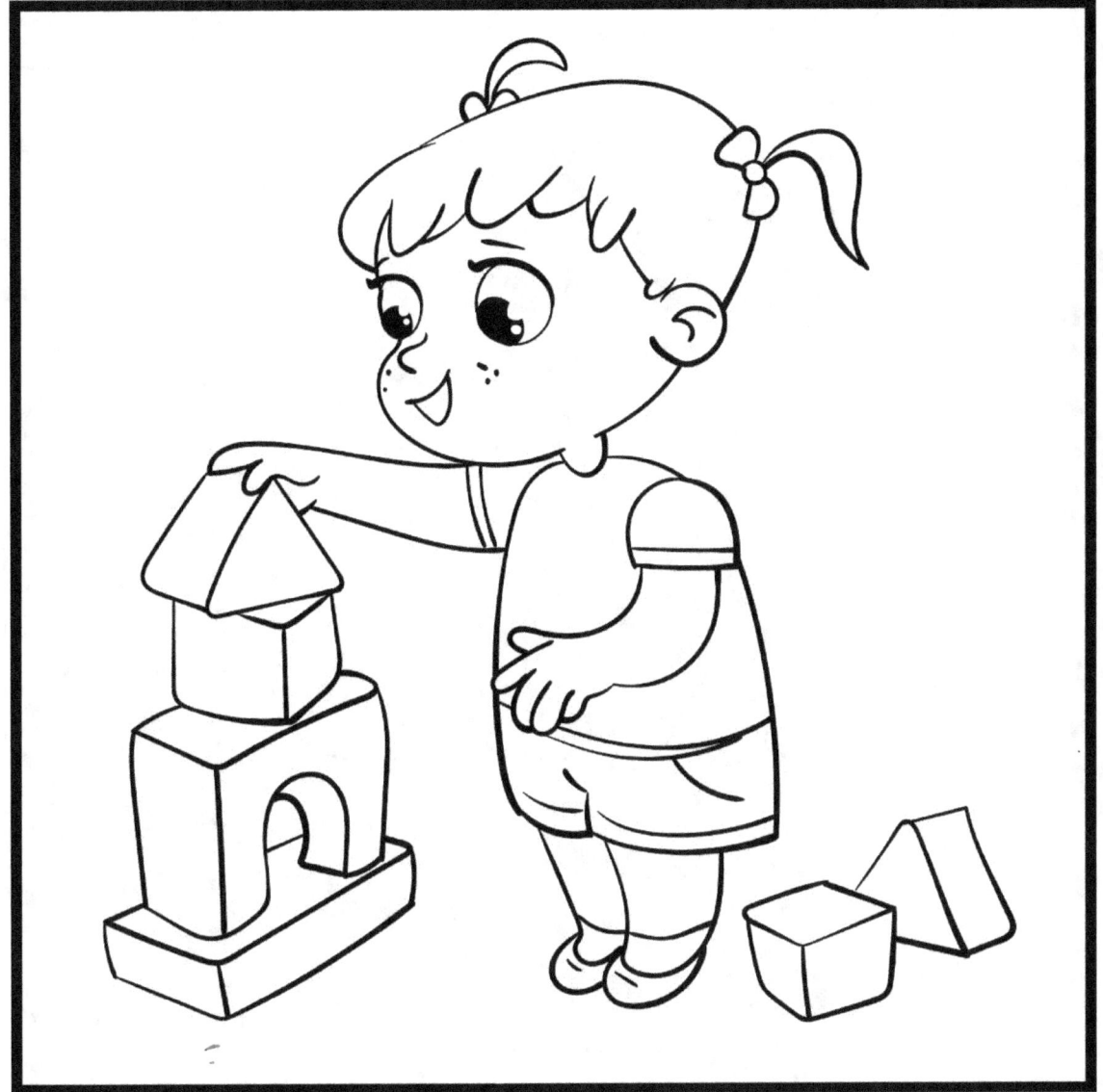

note:

_____

_____

_____

# OCTOBER 44TH

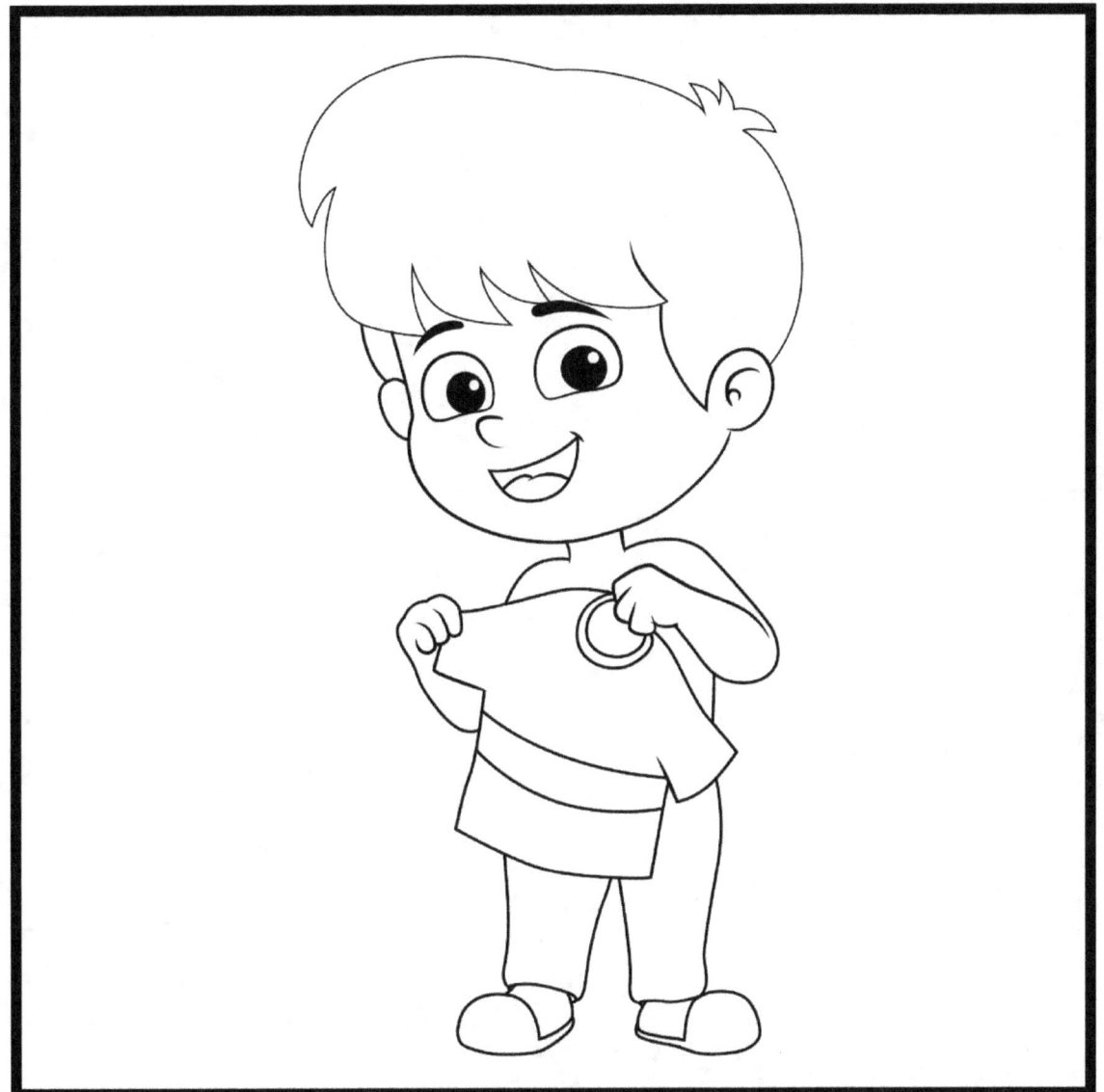

note:

_____

_____

_____

# OCTOBER 45TH

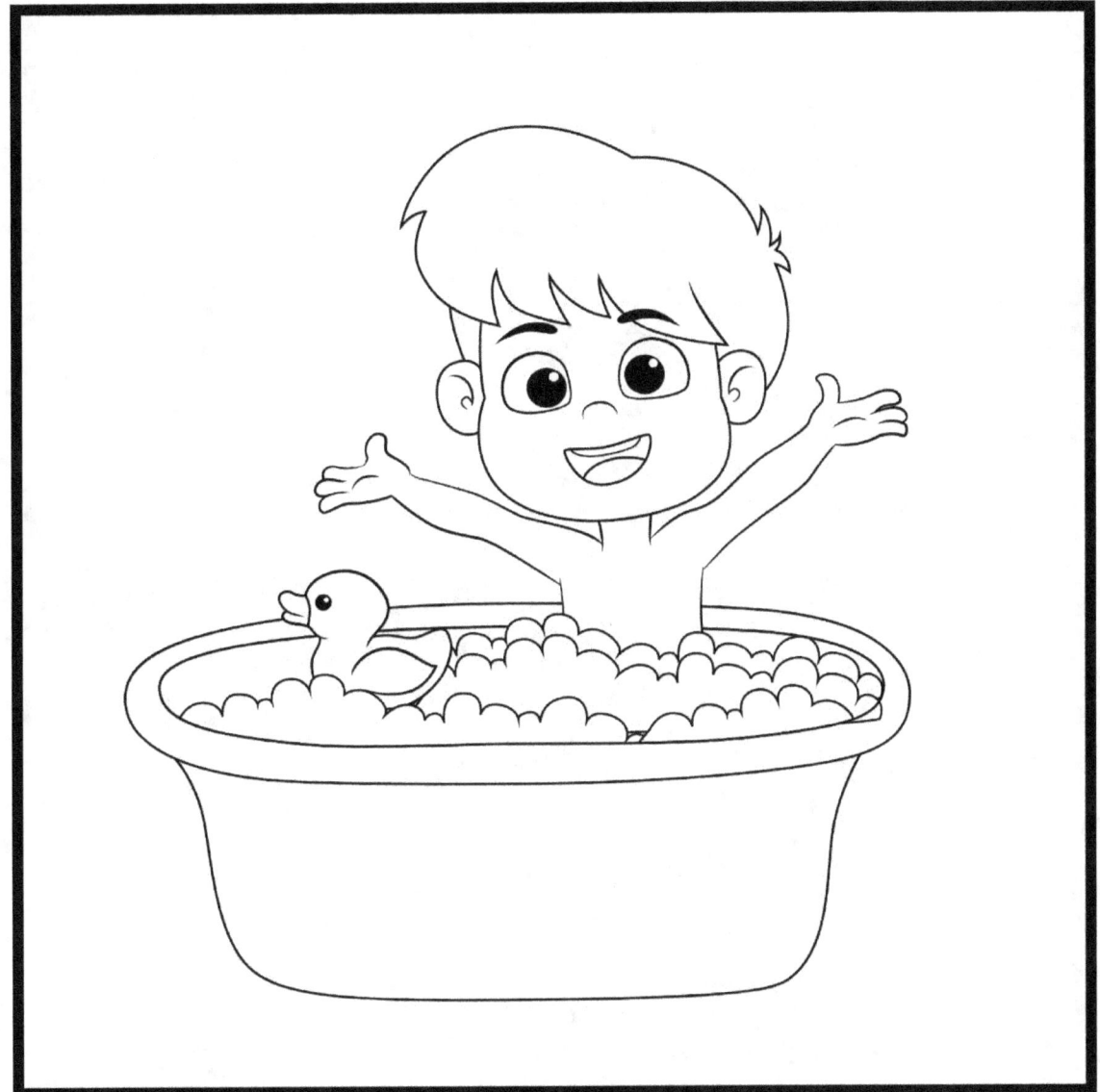

note:

_____

_____

_____

# OCTOBER 46TH

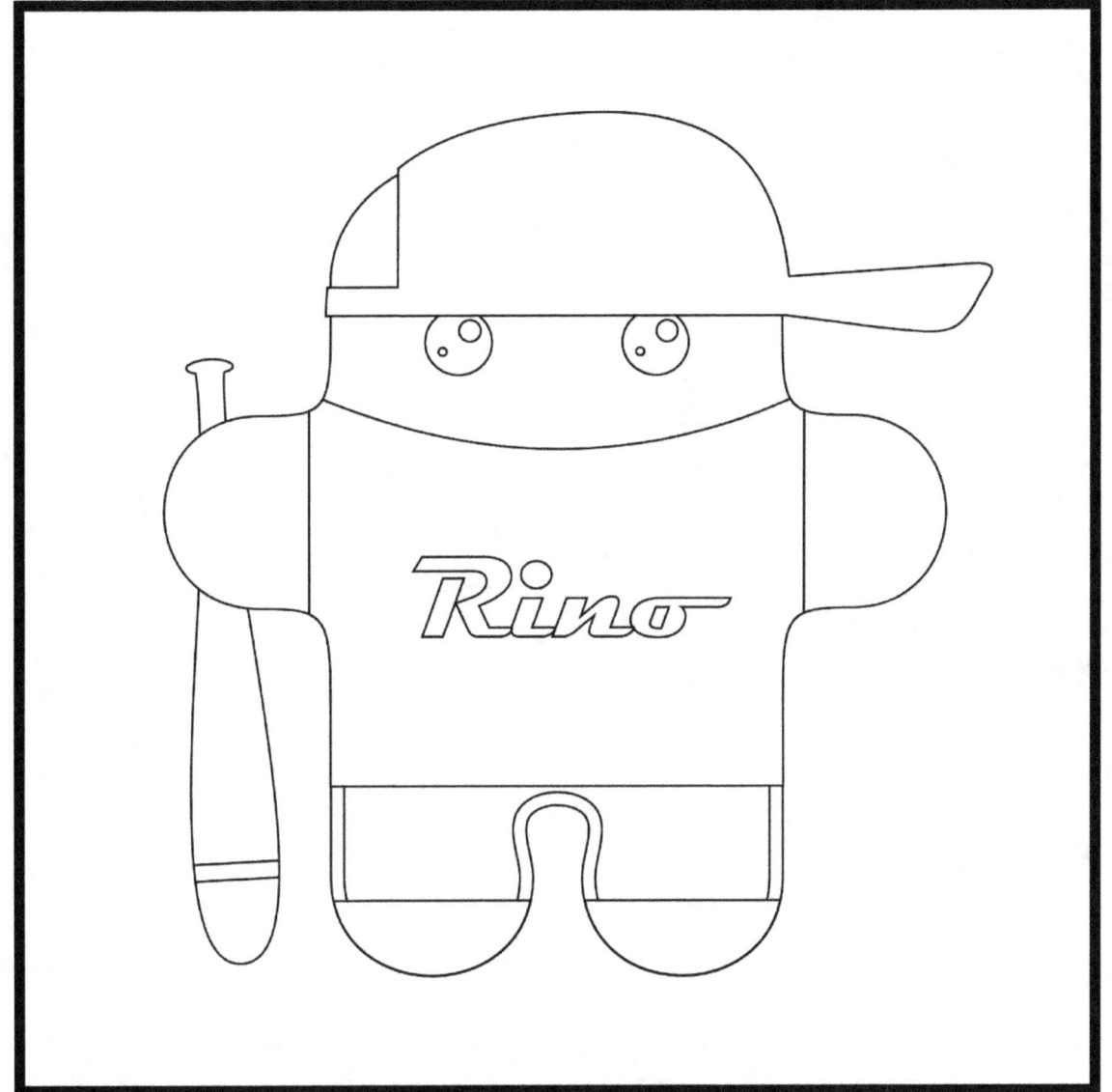

note:

_____

_____

_____

# OCTOBER 47TH

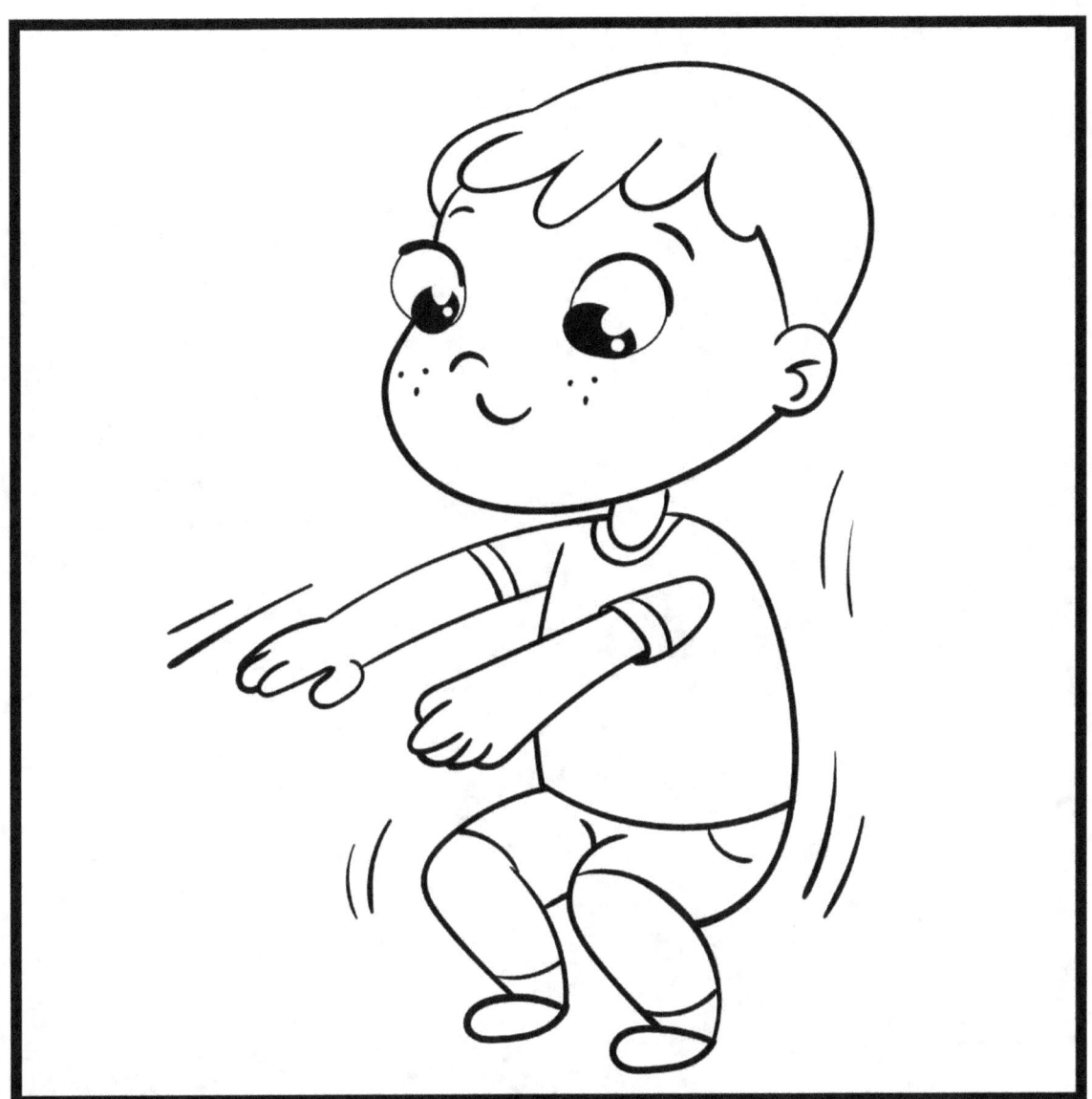

note:

_____

_____

_____

# OCTOBER 48TH

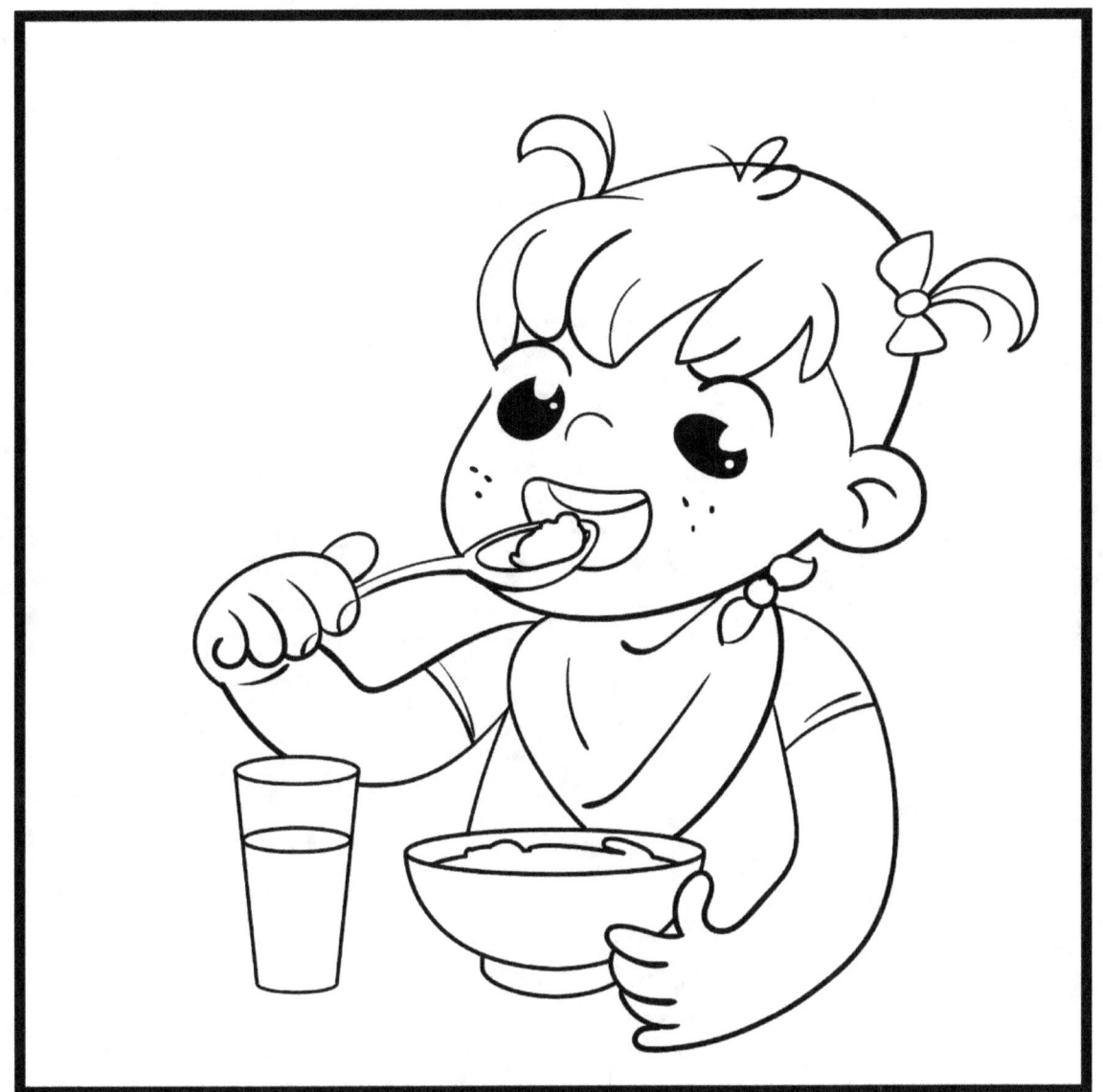

note:

_____

_____

_____

# OCTOBER 49TH

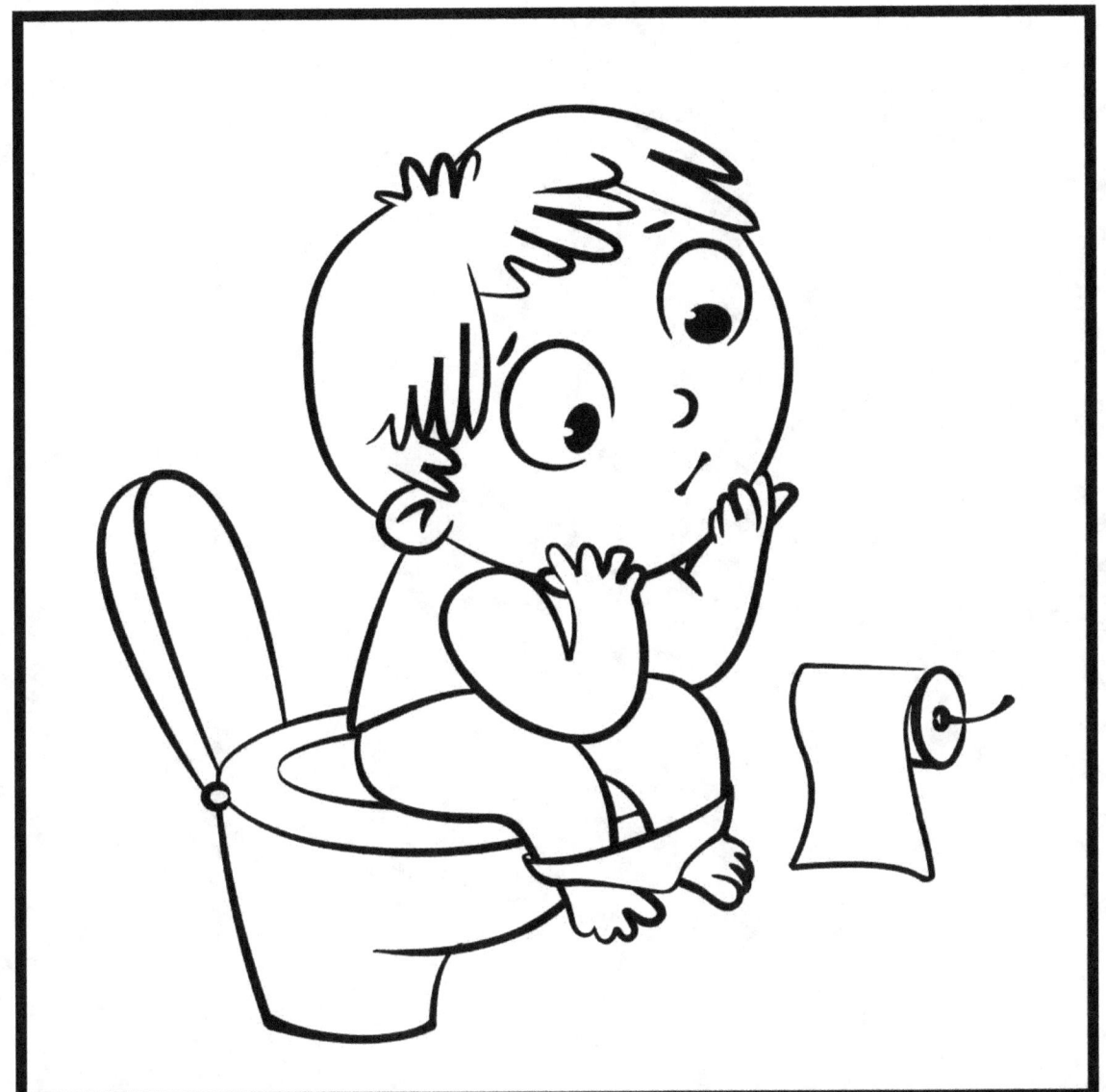

note:

_____

_____

_____

# OCTOBER 50TH

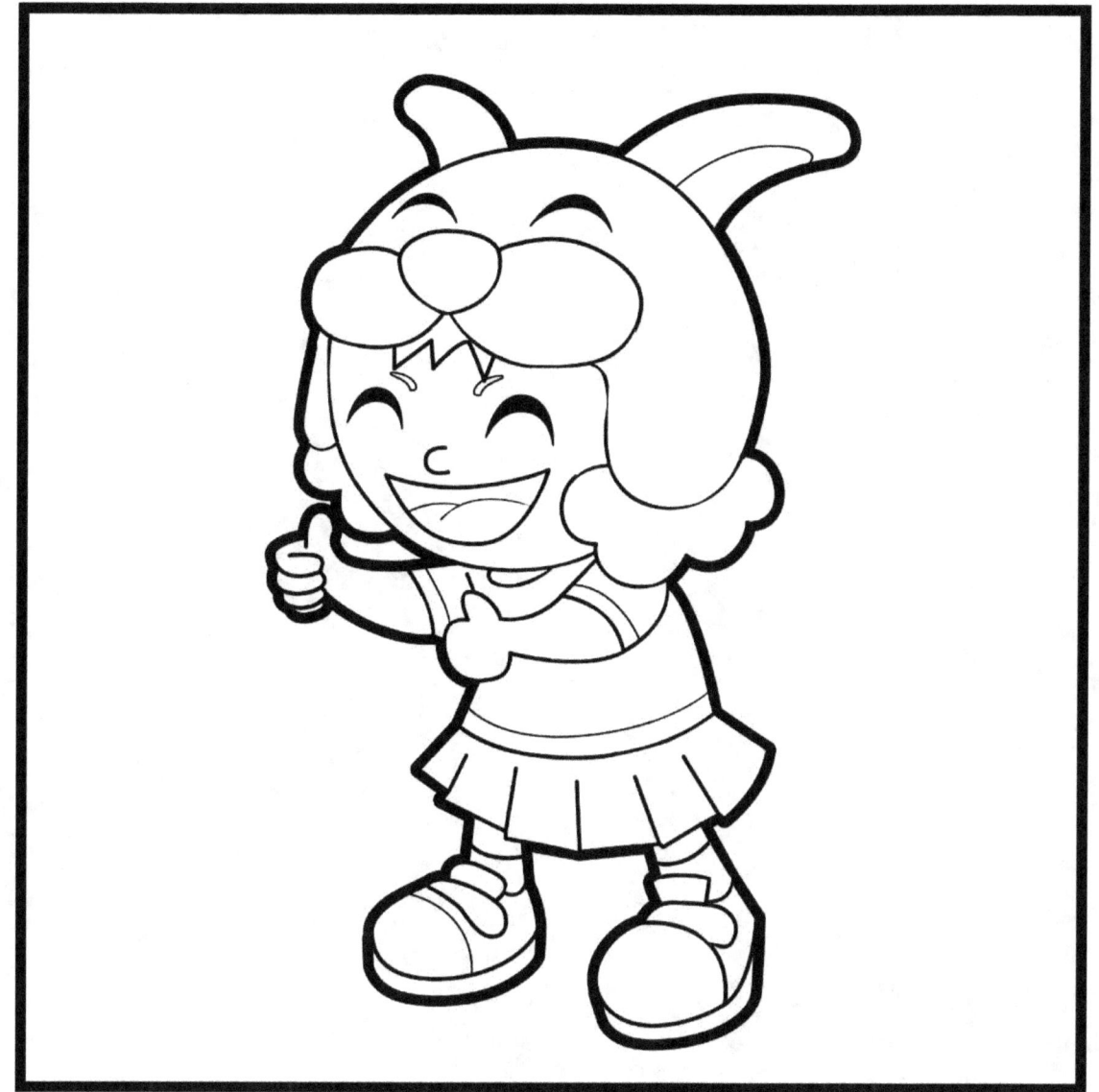

note:

_____

_____

_____